LAMB

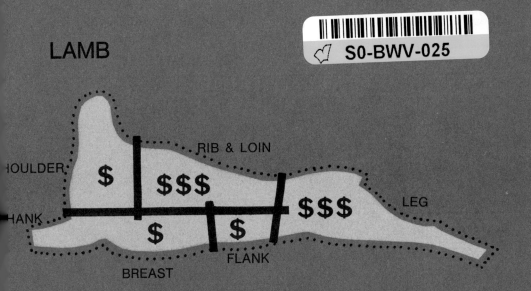

SHOULDER $

RIB & LOIN $$$

LEG

SHANK

$ BREAST

$ FLANK

$$$

PORK

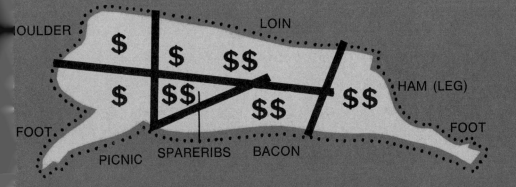

SHOULDER $

LOIN $ $$

HAM (LEG)

$ FOOT

$$ SPARERIBS

$$ BACON

$$ FOOT

PICNIC

The low-cost
meat book

THE LOW-COST
meat
BOOK

first-class fare
with economy meats

by

Nancy & Arthur Hawkins

illustrated by Arthur Hawkins

Doubleday & Company, Inc.
Garden City, New York 1973

ISBN #0-385-00401-x
Library of Congress Catalog Card Number 72-88707
Copyright © 1973 by Nancy and Arthur Hawkins
Printed in the United States of America
All Rights Reserved

1727685

We wish to acknowledge with thanks the generous assistance and co-operation of the following people:

Jean Anne Vincent of Doubleday for her indestructible confidence in the book from its inception.

Emil Buscher, meat manager of the Northern Valley Co-op in Leonia, New Jersey, and Charles Longfellow, New Jersey meat merchandiser and Robert Cusick meat manager (Engle-wood) of Food Fair, Inc. for their on-the-scene help in the identification and evaluation of economy meat cuts.

Monte R. Flett, director of merchandising of the National Live Stock and Meat Board, for invaluable advice and liter-ature on butchering, merchandising, and identifying meats.

To all of these people we are most grateful.

ILLUSTRATIONS

PRIME — United States Department of Agriculture Prime. (Pork is seldom graded because there is less variation in tenderness.) Animals thus stamped have been bred from the best stock, have been more carefully grazed and better fed. Comprising a minimal proportion of the market, *Prime* meats are not often available and invariably command the highest prices.

Meats labeled USDA CHOICE, only slightly inferior in quality to the top grade, make up the bulk of the supply in retail stores — perhaps as much as 75 per cent of the retail. Most of the remaining meats bear a label of USDA GOOD, an altogether acceptable quality but containing somewhat less fat, and therefore less flavor. Other meats, less often confronted, may be stamped USDA STANDARD or USDA COMMERCIAL.

Precarved meats usually appear in cuts too small to carry a grade stamp so you will usually find the package itself labeled.

Freshness   It is entirely possible that a piece of meat which has passed all the inspection tests for purity and quality may have been hanging around the butcher shop too long for its own good — or for yours. So always examine the meat you intend to buy with a critical eye — and nose. Fresh meat is firm, bright in color (not dark red), moist, and free from odor. If you detect a strong odor upon opening the package at home, wash the meat before assuming it is not fresh — the odor may merely have resulted from dried blood. The fat of fresh meat is creamy white (the whiter the better) and the suet is dry and crumbly. At today's meat prices there is no reason to accept any but the freshest.

Chops, cutlets, roasts, stay fresh from three to five days. Stew meat, hamburger, and variety meats, one or two days. Cured, smoked, and cooked meats, from three to seven days. If the meat you have on hand can't be used within these specified times, freeze it. Frozen small cuts will keep from two to three months, roasts and steaks from eight to twelve months. Freezing cured or cooked meats is not recommended because too much flavor is lost in the process.

Economy An advantage prepackaged meats have is that you can see exactly what you are going to get and how much you are paying per pound, and how much the cut of meat weighs. But you, alone, can be the judge of whether you are getting your money's worth. Carefully consider what proportion of the cut is edible, and what proportion is waste.

The price may be low but the bone may be big — and bone is surprisingly heavy. Many buyers prefer boneless cuts because they see exactly how much edible meat they are getting — and because boneless meats are easier to carve. Contrary to the old belief, the flavor of boneless meat is just as good.

The price may be low but the meat may contain a large proportion of tissue, gristle, and fat. Fat is a most desirable part of the meat; thin lines of fat marbling running throughout the meat makes it tender and flavorful, but too much fat is wasteful.

Buy the right amount of meat for your needs. Leftovers, without proper planning, will not always provide an extra meal and may not be economical. Unless there are some big appetites in the family, one pound of meat free from excess waste (fat, bone, etc.) should provide three servings.

There's one more important way you can beat high meat prices: Watch for special sales of specific cuts. Retail stores have to buy entire sides or quarters of meat from which they butcher the cuts you buy, and frequently they find themselves overstocked with one part or another because of changing demands. Thus, if you are careful and watchful, you may be able to pick up a porterhouse or sirloin steak, for example, priced below the so-called economy cuts. A good time to stock up the freezer compartment!

Which meat cuts to buy

*I*f you were to serve a different cut of meat—beef, veal, lamb, or pork—every day of the year, there would be variety enough to last a year without repeating menus. While all of the existing cuts are not carried by any one store, there is still a confusing assortment from which to choose.

To the economy minded, however, much of what you see in the market carries a pretty discouraging price tag. Only through knowledgeable shopping, therefore, can you maintain budget standards without sacrificing variety. It is, therefore, absolutely essential to learn something about meat identification—where the low-cost cuts come from, their relative cost, and how best to cook them.

In the American wholesale market, all meats are butchered "Chicago" style before shipping to retailers. Beef is split lengthwise into "sides" and then crosswise into "hindquarters" and "forequarters." Veal and lamb, because they are smaller, are not split lengthwise, but cut immediately into "hind saddle and fore saddle." (Pork, because of the many pork products processed at the packing plant—smoked hams,

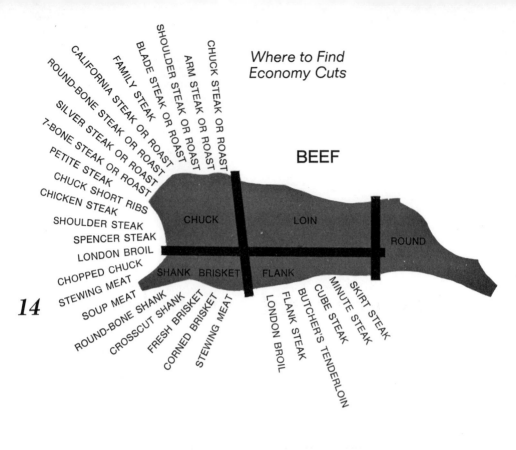

Where to Find Economy Cuts

BEEF

CHUCK STEAK OR ROAST
SHOULDER STEAK OR ROAST
ARM STEAK OR ROAST
BLADE STEAK OR ROAST
FAMILY STEAK
CALIFORNIA STEAK OR ROAST
ROUND-BONE STEAK OR ROAST
SILVER STEAK OR ROAST
7-BONE STEAK OR ROAST
PETITE STEAK
CHUCK SHORT RIBS
CHICKEN STEAK
SHOULDER STEAK
SPENCER STEAK
LONDON BROIL
CHOPPED CHUCK
STEWING MEAT
SOUP MEAT
ROUND-BONE SHANK
CROSSCUT SHANK
FRESH BRISKET
CORNED BRISKET
STEWING MEAT
LONDON BROIL
FLANK STEAK
BUTCHER'S TENDERLOIN
CUBE STEAK
MINUTE STEAK
SKIRT STEAK

CHUCK
LOIN
ROUND
SHANK BRISKET
FLANK

14

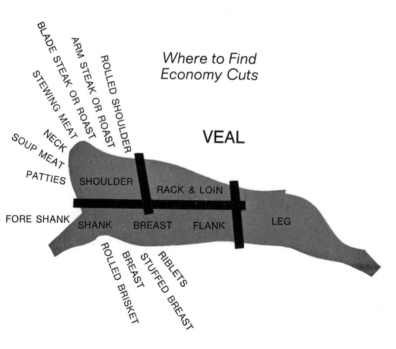

Where to Find Economy Cuts

VEAL

BLADE STEAK OR ROAST
ARM STEAK OR ROAST
ROLLED SHOULDER
STEWING MEAT
NECK
SOUP MEAT
PATTIES
FORE SHANK
RIBLETS
STUFFED BREAST
BREAST
ROLLED BRISKET

SHOULDER
RACK & LOIN
SHANK
BREAST
FLANK
LEG

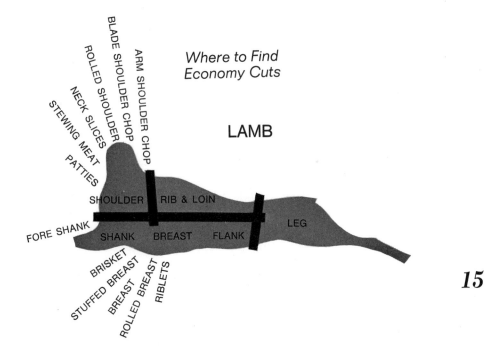

Where to Find
Economy Cuts

LAMB

STEWING MEAT
NECK SLICES
ROLLED SHOULDER
BLADE SHOULDER CHOP
ARM SHOULDER CHOP
PATTIES

SHOULDER   RIB & LOIN

FORE SHANK   SHANK   BREAST   FLANK   LEG

BRISKET
STUFFED BREAST
BREAST
ROLLED BREAST
RIBLETS

15

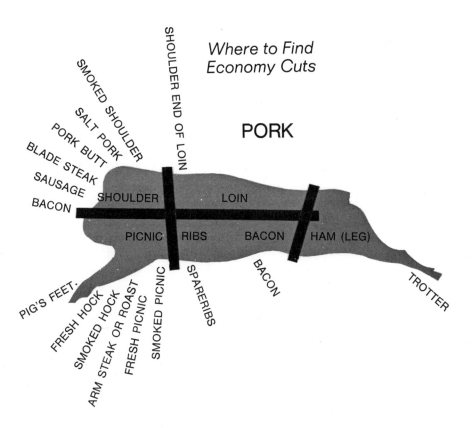

Where to Find
Economy Cuts

PORK

SMOKED SHOULDER
SALT PORK
PORK BUTT
BLADE STEAK
SAUSAGE
BACON
SHOULDER END OF LOIN

SHOULDER   LOIN

PICNIC   RIBS   BACON   HAM (LEG)

PIG'S FEET:
FRESH HOCK
SMOKED HOCK
ARM STEAK OR ROAST
FRESH PICNIC
SMOKED PICNIC
SPARERIBS
BACON
TROTTER

sausages, bacon, lamb, etc. — is butchered according to an entirely different formula.) The "quarters" or "saddles" are then subdivided into leg (or round), loin, short loin, rib, shoulder and neck (chuck), shank, plate, and flank.

So far, so good. But now the plot thickens, because your local butcher now gets to work on the eight "primal" cuts just mentioned and slices them into all sorts of morsels. Then he trims them, weighs them, packages them, and gives them names — names like "chicken steak" (if you are a Philadelphian, you've never heard of such a cut because there it goes under the name of "petite steak"), or "London broil" — unknown on the Pacific coast, and a vague designation anywhere since it may come from the round, loin, or chuck. The chart on page 14, which lists some of the names the various cuts are marketed under, will show you what you are up against.

In some stores the origin of the cut is indicated on the package and in some localities the law requires specific labeling. If the information you need is not on the package, ask for it. You've got to know! You've got to know which part of the animal the meat you are buying has been taken from, because only then will you know how to cook it. Meat is muscle. Muscles the animal uses the least are the tenderest and usually, but not always, contain the most fat (and usually, but not always, are the most expensive). And there is a surprising difference in the flavor of cuts taken from forequarter and hindquarter, from rib and shank.

If you are shopping economy, you will select cuts taken from the forequarters of the animal, avoiding those from the loin and round or rump. If you are an Orthodox Jew, this will of course be easy since only forequarter meat is sold in kosher stores — except in Israel where, due to the scarcity of meat of any kind, specially trained butchers remove the veins and arteries making even the hindquarters acceptable.

Be sure not to overlook the so-called variety meats — liver, kidneys, heart, sweetbreads, brains, tongue, and tripe. All these qualify as economy meats — no bone, no waste — are excellent sources of many essential nutrients, and can be cooked and served in many interesting ways. And then there are the sausages — beef frankfurters, fresh pork sausages, smoked sausages, bratwurst, knackwurst, Polish sausage, Italian sausage, bologna, salami, liverwurst, etc.

There are plenty of meats available for the economy-minded shopper, and there are plenty of delicious meals to be made from them, all you have to do is try a little harder—care a little more.

17

Tenderizing, marinating, and larding

All meats can't be tender and succulent. Muscles of the animal that are most active often yield cuts that are grainy and interlaced with tissue. This meat can be flavorful, but before serving it, you will either have to moist-heat cook it a long time or give it some sort of treatment before cooking.

There are several such treatments:

TENDERIZING

You can apply a chemical tenderizer. Available from most food stores, this product resembles and tastes like ordinary table salt, which it contains along with sucrose. But the tenderizing effect derives from another ingredient—an enzyme extracted from the papayan melon. This tenderizer is easy to use. You simply sprinkle it evenly onto all the surfaces of the meat, which are then pierced generously with a fork to insure penetration into the inner portions. Allow the meat to stand for half an hour or so at room temperature (longer if thick) and cook according to the recipe you have decided upon. Most chemical tenderizers do not flavor the meat, but there are some brands that contain seasonings and spices. All, however, are well fortified with salt so no additional salt need be added. A word of caution when using any tenderizer: Don't overdo, too much enzyme working too long will result in mushy meat.

Soon after the discovery of papaya as a tenderizing agent, an enterprising meat processor conceived of injecting steers with papaya fluid a short time before slaughtering, reasoning that the tenderizer would be carried in the bloodstream to all parts of the body. According to the story, the plan worked. Too well! All parts of the steer were tenderized, but the effect was equal throughout and the tenderer morsels of the meat were too soft to eat.

A second method of tenderizing—by far the most prevalent—is purely mechanical. The tough connecting tissues are broken down simply by pounding. For this there are many gadgets available—spiked mallets of all shapes and sizes, implements with needles, and complicated assortments of steel blades—but you can achieve the same results by using the edge of a plate. If the pounding flattens the meat more than you would like, try doing as your butcher does with cube steaks. Take a sharp knife and crosshatch on both sides with light, close-together incisions and the tissues will be effectively broken down without disfiguring the meat.

French butchers at one time used an ingenious machine consisting of hundreds of sharp needles that penetrated the meat and successfully tenderized it, but the machine, difficult to keep clean, was discovered to contribute to the spread of botulism. The tenderizer was outlawed.

MARINATING

Some cuts of meat, though tender enough to broil may seem tasteless—lacking in flavor. Try a marinade. It's easy and effective. Place the meat into a non-metallic receptacle just large enough to contain it and pour in enough marinating mixture to cover it completely. Put a lid on the dish and place it into the refrigerator for an hour or so (or overnight), stirring from time to time. Remove the meat and broil in the prescribed manner, brushing with some of the marinade as it cooks.

There are many marinating mixtures, each imparting its own flavor, but most of them contain an acid—either wine, vinegar, or lemon—to break down the connecting tissues, an oil of some sort, spices, and seasonings. Some contain vegetables. The simplest and quickest marinade you can make is an oil and vinegar mix (three parts oil to one part vinegar) known everywhere as French dressing. You can use a prepared French dressing too.

The following recipes will get you started, after which you might like to invent your own more elaborate marinades according to your own taste. The quantities of ingredients given are for meat cuts averaging two pounds. Increase quantities proportionately for a larger cut.

Vinegar Marinade for Beef

Mix together:
1/2 **cup olive oil or vegetable oil**
1/2 **cup tarragon vinegar**
1 **carrot, minced**
1 **onion, minced**
3 **sprigs parsley**
1 **bay leaf**
1 **teaspoon salt**
1 **teaspoon pepper**

Wine Marinade for Beef

Mix together:
1/2 **cup dry red wine**
1/2 **cup vegetable oil or olive oil**
1 **onion, chopped**
1 **clove garlic, chopped**
1 **teaspoon dried herbs, such as rosemary, thyme, or marjoram**
1/2 **cup chopped parsley**
few drops Tabasco
1 **teaspoon salt**

Wine Marinade for Lamb and Veal

Mix together:
$1/2$ cup dry white wine or vermouth
$1/2$ cup vegetable oil or olive oil
2 tablespoons lemon juice
1 large onion, chopped
1 teaspoon salt
1 teaspoon freshly ground pepper

Vinegar Marinade for Lamb and Veal

Mix together:
1 cup French dressing
1 onion, chopped
1 clove garlic, chopped
1 bay leaf
4 sprigs parsley
pinch dried tarragon
pinch thyme
1 teaspoon salt
1 teaspoon pepper

Marinade for Spareribs

Mix together:
1 teaspoon cornstarch
1 cup vinegar
1 teaspoon sugar
1 cup sherry
1 teaspoon soy sauce
2 teaspoons salt

LARDING

There are times when you may be confronted with a very lean cut of meat, usually beef or veal, that you wish to roast. The heat of the oven will most certainly dry out the meat by the time it is properly cooked. The solution is, of course, to add fat. Have the butcher thread a strip of fat salt pork through the meat, or if you have a larding needle, you can do it yourself. Or do it the easy (though less effective) way and lay strips of fat or bacon across the top of the roast.

Be your own butcher 23
— and save

*L*ook into the meat bin of your favorite market and you will find a sizable variety of small precarved cuts already packaged and ready to take home: petite steaks (sometimes called chicken steaks), Saratoga steaks, shoulder steaks, chuck fillets, flanken, cubes of beef, lamb, and veal for stewing, and chops of all kinds — just to name a few. All of these, of course, have been cut by the butcher from larger pieces of meat. And they sell at a higher price, the total revenue from all the small cuts being greater than that of the large cut from which they were taken.

You can butcher your own small cuts and save, all you will need is a good sharp knife and a little ingenuity. Here are an even half dozen money-saving plans to start you off. All involve buying a bit more meat than you need for one meal and, instead of being stuck with leftovers, ending up with several, fresh-cooked and entirely different meals.

Money-Saver #1 (7 servings)

Buy 2 2-pound USDA Choice flat-bone chuck steaks, about 1 inch thick.

First, remove the petite steaks (chicken steaks) (1) leaving them edged with a bit of fat. Then cut out the chuck fillets. (2) Pan-broil these 4 tender little steaks and serve them as your first meal. They will provide 3 generous servings.

Cut the rest of the meat (3) into cubes, put together with vegetables and make a beef stew (see Index) and you will have enough for two meals for two (4 servings).

Simmer the bones in enough water to cover, season to taste, and in an hour or so strain off the broth and use for making soup.

24

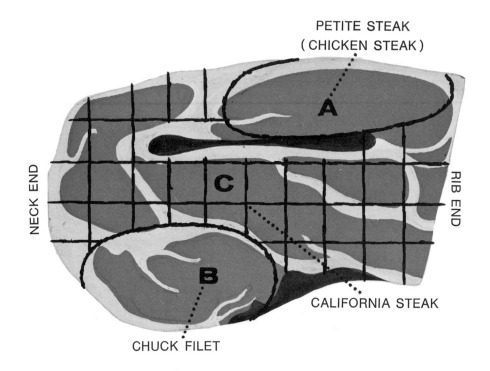

CHUCK BLADE STEAK

Money-Saver #2 (8 servings)

Buy 2 2-pound USDA Choice 7-bone chuck steaks about 1 inch thick.

Remove the chicken steaks(1) — they will be smaller on this cut than on the flat-bone chuck — and the Saratoga steaks(2). Pan-broil for meal number one, 2 servings.

Slice off the neck end of the steaks (3), put through the meat grinder, and you'll have enough for 4 good-size hamburgers — meals numbers two and three (4 servings).

Pound flour into the remaining steaks (4), using the edge of a plate, and cook as Swiss steaks (see Index). These will serve 2 for meal number four.

And once again, don't forget about simmering the bones.

25

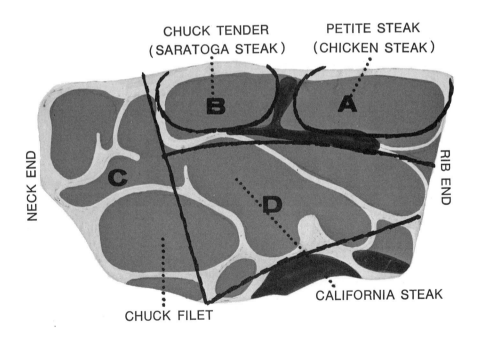

CHUCK TENDER (SARATOGA STEAK) PETITE STEAK (CHICKEN STEAK)

NECK END

RIB END

B A

C

D

CALIFORNIA STEAK

CHUCK FILET

CHUCK 7-BONE STEAK

Money-Saver #3 (8 servings)

Buy 2 1-inch Choice arm chuck steaks (full cut), weighing about 2 pounds each. You might not always be able to find this cut, since chuck is butchered differently in different sections of the country—even in different stores.

Remove the shoulder steaks (1) and pan-broil—dish number one, 2 servings.

Remove the briskets (2), braise, and you have dish number two, 2 servings.

Cut the rest of the meat into cubes (3) for a stew (see Index), making dish number three which will provide 4 servings.

26

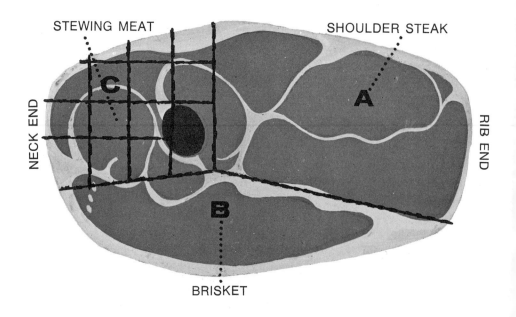

CHUCK ARM STEAK

Money-Saver #4 (6 servings)

Buy 2 1-inch sirloin or porterhouse steaks. (If you watch the newspaper ads, you can often catch them on sale). Pick out a couple with lean tails.

Have the butcher grind the tails (1) which will make meal number one of top quality hamburger, 2 servings.

The steaks (2) will each serve 2 and you will have meals numbers two and three, 4 servings.

Three meals for 2 for the price of two!

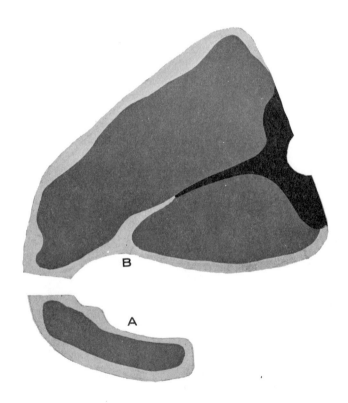

Money-Saver #5 (10 servings)

Ham is not exactly economy fare but there is a way of extending it over several meals and therefore cutting down on the cost.

Buy the shank half of a smoked ham and have your butcher saw off the shank end(1). There's lots of flavor in this piece which you can bring out by simmering with onions, potatoes, and carrots. Cook until the meat almost falls from the bone and you will have a mighty nice "boiled" dinner, dish number one, which should serve 4, depending upon size.

Carve the remaining part into 2 pieces, cutting along the hip bone. Bake the bone-in piece (2) in a preheated 325 degrees F. oven and carve off small slice — dish number two, 2 large servings.

The remaining portion (3) is carved — against the grain — into 4 steaks which may be pan-broiled and served with pineapple (see Index), and which should make up dishes numbers three and four, 4 servings.

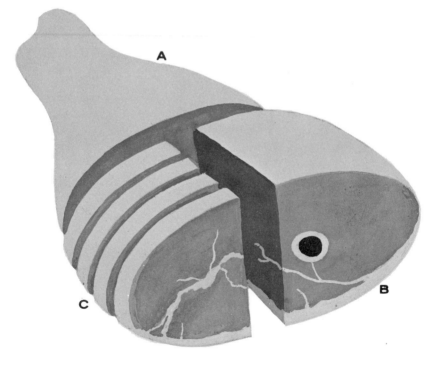

Money-Saver #6 (12 servings)

A large leg of lamb can become almost an economy cut if you prebutcher it instead of cooking it all at once and serving leftovers.

You'll need a bone saw, or you can have your butcher saw it up as illustrated here.

The 4 steaks (1) will serve 4—dish number one.

The center portion (2), oven roasted at 325 degrees F. will provide generous helpings for 4 at a second meal—dish number two.

Later in the week cut cubes of meat from the shank (3) and use for a stew or kebobs (see Index) and you'll have dish number three.

Three generous meals for 4 people from a large leg of lamb!

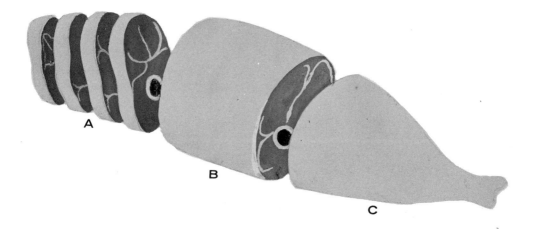

A

B

C

Cooking meat:
let the method fit the cut

Anybody can cook meat. All you do is apply heat. But just *how* you apply the heat to the particular cut of meat you have on hand can spell the difference between a satisfying and imaginative meal and an indifferent one.

The following are the methods. All cooks know them all. But which method for which cut? Ah, that is the question!

ROASTING

Roasting — using dry oven heat — is the best method of cooking large tender cuts of meat.

Place the meat, fat side up, into a shallow roasting pan and cook in an oven preheated to 325 degrees F. (350 degrees for pork). Cook to desired doneness. Do not sprinkle with flour, do not add water, do not baste. As the fat melts, it will moisten the meat. If the meat is very lean, toothpick a piece of suet, bacon, or salt pork to the top.

The cooking time will depend upon the thickness and leanness of the meat. To eliminate all guesswork, insert a cooking thermometer into an incision made in the center of the meat, making certain that it does not rest against the bone. When the meat is done, the dial will show the temperature—beef: 140 degrees for rare, 160 degrees for medium, and 170 degrees for well done; lamb: 175 degrees for medium and 180 degrees for well done; veal should be cooked at 180 degrees and pork at 185 degrees.

Some economy meats suitable for roasting:

beef brisket (top quality)	breast of veal
beef rump roast	rolled shoulder of lamb
beef short ribs	breast of lamb
beef London broil (sirloin)	shoulder of pork (butt)
veal shank half of leg	rolled leg of pork
veal rolled shoulder	loin of pork
rolled shoulder of veal	pork spareribs

BROILING

Broiling is a dry heat method of cooking by direct heat. You can broil on top of the stove using a skillet, or in the broiling compartment of your oven, or over charcoal.

To pan-broil, place the meat in a preheated heavy skillet and cook on both sides to desired doneness. Do not add fat (if the meat is lean, a little salt in the skillet will prevent sticking). Do not cover. Pour off any excess fat as it accumulates (or the meat will fry). Cook according to recipe specifications. This is the time-saver method—and there's no oven to clean, either.

To oven-broil, preheat the broiler compartment and grease the broiler rack to prevent sticking. Line the broiler pan with foil, if you wish, to save washing. Place the meat onto the rack and position about 2 inches from the heat. Cook half the specified time on one side, turn and complete on the other.

To charcoal-broil, place meat onto a greased grill and position 2 or 3 inches from white-hot coals (coals covered uniformly with a white ash) according to recipe. Dripping fat may catch fire and char the meat. The flames may be extinguished, if you desire, by spraying lightly with water.

Some economy meats suitable for broiling:

beef flank steak	lamb patties
beef skirt steak	pork sausage patties
beef flanken	pork arm steak
beef shoulder steak	pork blade steak
beef London broil (sirloin)	pork spareribs
beef chicken steak (petite steak)	ham slices
beef hamburger	bacon
veal patties	beef, veal, and lamb liver
	veal and lamb kidneys
	sweetbreads

SAUTÉING

Sautéing (sometimes called pan-frying) is a dry method of cooking similar to pan-broiling.

To sauté heat 3 or 4 tablespoons of fat in a frying pan, when fat bubbles add the meat (floured or not according to recipe) and brown on both sides. Add other ingredients, seasonings, and liquid called for by recipe and continue to cook over medium heat until meat is done and sauce, if any, is reduced to half. If the meat is floured, the sauce will not need thickening. Sautéing combines the best of pan-frying and braising.

Some economy meats suitable for sautéing:

thin-cut beef steaks	veal and lamb kidneys
beef, veal, lamb liver	brains
sweetbreads	

BRAISING

Braising is a most heat method used for cooking less tender cuts of meat.

To braise, brown the meat in a heavy skillet using a small amount of fat or oil if the meat is lean. Predust with flour, if you wish. Add liquid (water, vinegar or wine, lemon or tomato juice, stock, etc.) according to recipe, cover tightly, and cook at low temperature either on top of the stove or in a moderate (350 degree) oven. Acid liquids, such as vinegar, wine, fruit juices, have a tenderizing effect by breaking down connective tissue.

Since the liquid absorbs some of the meat flavor, use it to make a gravy or sauce.

Some economy meats suitable for braising:

beef arm steak (short cut)	breast of lamb
beef blade steak (full cut)	lamb neck slices
beef short ribs	pork blade steak
beef English (Boston) cut	brains
veal blade steak	heart
breast of veal	kidneys
lamb shank	sweetbreads

COOKING IN LIQUID

Less tender cuts of meat are best cooked in liquid by either stewing or "boiling."

To stew, place the meat into a pot with sufficient liquid to cover, and simmer slowly until tender. The liquid may be water, stock, wine, tomato juice, etc., or a combination of liquids. Use the liquid to make a sauce or gravy. Stewing is the method used to make a fricassee, ragout, or pot roast.

In boiling, the liquid used is always water—and you don't really *boil* the meat, you *simmer* it. Since the purpose is to break down the less tender tissues of the meat, simmering at low temperature in a covered pot for a longer period of time will generally result in greater tenderness. Most meats require at least 2 hours of gentle simmering.

Some economy meats suitable for cooking in liquid:

fresh brisket of beef	smoked picnic (butt)
corned beef	fresh pork hocks
beef for stew	smoked pork hocks
veal fore shank	fresh pigs' feet
breast of veal	fresh country-style ribs
veal for stew	beef heart
lamb for stew	sweetbreads
breast of lamb	tongue
pork spareribs	tripe

PRESSURE COOKING

A pressure cooker can save a good two-thirds of the time necessary to cook meat, because it cooks by steam pressure built up in the cooker and contained by the strong construction of the cooker. The steam is also contained by a sealing ring, a pressure regulator, and an automatic air vent. The instructions that come with the cooker should be studied carefully. There are a few basic rules that should not be disregarded in the use of a cooker. Once these are mastered a pressure cooker will pay for itself in the time it saves tenderizing and cooking tough meats.

It is best used for stews, pot roasts, economy cuts for roasts such as rump, top, bottom, sirloin, roasts, veal roasts, and pork roasts. All roasts should be seared in the cooker to brown before they are put under pressure, and water must be added to produce the steam.

Proteins — the staff of intelligence

Recent studies have shown that not only physical but mental development is affected by lack of proteins in the diet of young children, particularly during periods of fast growth. Babies and nursing and pregnant women require high protein consumption, as do teen-agers during periods of growth. Two or more servings per day of meat or other high protein food give all the protein needed per person.

Meat is first-class protein that contains an abundance of all eight essential amino acids. In this category are eggs, meat, fish, and milk. The second-class proteins are limited by a relative, though seldom complete, absence of one of the essential amino acids, for example vegetable proteins and those of cereals and legumes. But one protein can make up for a lack of an amino acid in another by compensating for a deficiency in another. The value of wheat protein is much less than the value of milk protein, but the total protein in bread and milk is very close to that of milk itself because the deficiency of lysine in the cereal protein is compensated for by the excess of this amino acid in milk protein, which makes a better food value than either separately.

Well-chewed meat is better digested, and nutrients are more completely absorbed by the body.

The following quantities of meats will fill one fourth of the day's protein needs:

steak, hamburger, or other boneless meats ... $\frac{1}{5}$ pound
steaks, chops, roasts, or other medium-boned
    meats .... $\frac{1}{4}$ pound
ribs, breast, shanks, or other much-boned
    meats .... $\frac{1}{4}$ to $\frac{1}{2}$ pound
pork sausages .... $\frac{1}{4}$ to $\frac{1}{2}$ pound
frankfurters .... $2\frac{1}{2}$
1-ounce slices bologna 4
bacon slices .... 6 to 8

Meat extenders:
more nutrition, less cost

Meat is the most costly item in the food budget. The reason for this is that animal husbandry is the most costly way to produce food. Even though 2 or 3 ounces of meat might be an adequate amount of protein to serve, such an amount does not yield a very big serving.

Institutions, and some restaurants too, use synthetic meat substitutes made from soybean protein to add bulk to meat dishes. Although USDA has approved 30 per cent of these substitutes for institutional and school use, they are still inferior to meat both in flavor and texture. It will require many more years of experimentation with these substances to achieve really satisfactory results. No one knows for sure what values existing in meat are not contained in the substitutes, even though they might be high in protein. As things stand now, you must be guided by taste and good judgment.

But there are, fortunately, other ways to extend the quantity of meat—and save money. You can add a second, less-expensive meat, or seafood, or cheese, or eggs, or a stuffing, or other lesser proteins such as beans and nuts.

Following are some suggestions for extending meats and cutting costs:

Meat Extender #1: A Second Meat

Grilled Lamb Chops with Kidneys

(4 SERVINGS)

4 loin lamb chops
4 lamb kidneys
4 slices bacon
4 slices buttered toast with crusts trimmed
¼ teaspoon salt
¼ teaspoon pepper

Preheat broiler to 400 degrees F.

Trim excess fat from chops and center fat from kidneys. Soak or parboil the kidneys to reduce the flavor, or use as is. Skewer to the chop in the curve of the bone.

Wrap slices of bacon around the kidney-chops and secure with skewers or string.

Place into a shallow pan, sprinkle with salt and pepper, slide under the broiler, and cook 6 minutes on each side or until well browned. Serve on buttered toast.

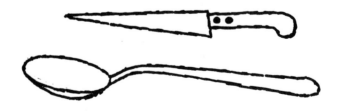

Beef Roulades

(4 SERVINGS)

1 pound sausage meat
1 onion, chopped
2 slices stale bread, wet, wrung out, and crum-
bled
¼ teaspoon thyme
½ teaspoon salt
¼ teaspoon pepper
4 tablespoons flour
4 thin slices of top round 12 x 4 inches, pounded
4 small pickles
1 cup consommé

Put the sausage meat into a heavy skillet, and cook at medium-low heat, breaking the meat up as it cooks.

Add the onion and, when it is golden, put in the crumbled bread and the seasonings. Stir together.

Flour the roulades lightly and spoon an even amount of the sausage mixture onto each. Add a pickle, roll up, and tie with a string.

Return to the skillet and brown on all sides. Add the consommé, lower the heat, and simmer about 20 minutes.

Stuffed Breast of Veal

(4 SERVINGS)

**3 pounds breast of veal
salt
pepper
2 cups bread stuffing
3 slices salt pork or bacon
1 cup beef bouillon or stock
flour
water**

Preheat oven to 325 degrees F.

Remove the large bones from the veal with a boning knife (or have your butcher do it for you), pat dry with a paper towel, and season with salt and pepper.

Cover half the meat with stuffing, fold over the rest of the meat, and skewer together.

Place onto the rack of a baking pan, greased to prevent sticking. Cover with slices of salt pork, pour the bouillon over all, and cover the pan.

Bake about 2½ to 3 hours, uncover and cook ½ hour longer, and remove to a heated serving platter.

Thicken the broth with a little flour and water, pour over the meat, and serve.

Pork Chops with Sausages

(4 SERVINGS)

**4 loin pork chops
4 large sausages (8, if small)
1 tablespoon flour
½ cup water
½ teaspoon salt
¼ teaspoon pepper**

Brown the chops in a heavy skillet over high heat. Reduce the heat, add the sausages, and cook together about 20 minutes, turning the sausages as they brown.

Remove meats to a warm platter, and pour off all the fat except 1 tablespoon. Add the flour, let brown a little, add water, and stir well. Serve each chop with a sausage and a spoonful of gravy.

Veal and Kidney Stew

(6 SERVINGS)

3 tablespoons bacon fat or vegetable oil
2 veal kidneys, with fat removed and cut same size as meat
1½ pounds veal stew meat
5 tablespoons flour
1 teaspoon salt
½ teaspoon pepper
1 onion, sliced thin
3 cups water or bouillon

Heat the bacon fat in a heavy skillet and add the fat cut from the kidneys. Dredge the veal and kidneys with flour, season with salt and pepper, and add to the skillet. Brown well on all sides.

Add the onion and stir until golden, then pour in the water and stir to get brown up from bottom of the pan. Cover, leaving a vent for the steam, and simmer 1½ hours, or until meat is tender. Add more water if gravy gets too thick.

You can use beef in place of veal. Fats must be removed from beef kidneys. If the kidney flavor is too strong for you, parboil them in a little water for a few minutes.

Lamb Kabobs

All over Athens there are tiny outdoor "restaurants" operating with charcoal stoves. Cubes of lamb that have been well marinated in olive oil, lemon juice, garlic, and various seasonings are skewered onto slivers of bamboo and charcoal-broiled until black-brown. You stop, buy two or three—or four—and eat them standing there. Mmmm . . .

(4 SERVINGS)

1¹⁄₂ pounds lamb shoulder, cut into 1-inch cubes
marinade (see Index)
4 slices bacon, cut into quarters
¹⁄₂ pound button mushrooms*
1 teaspoon salt
¹⁄₂ teaspoon pepper

Place the lamb cubes into a shallow dish and cover with a good marinade containing garlic. Cover, place in the refrigerator, and let stand over night. (Or marinate at room temperature for 2 to 3 hours.)

Alternate lamb, bacon, and mushrooms on metal skewers. Season with salt and pepper, and broil, turning, a few inches away from heat for about 15 minutes or until done.

° Lamb kidneys or liver cut into 1-inch cubes may be used instead of mushrooms.

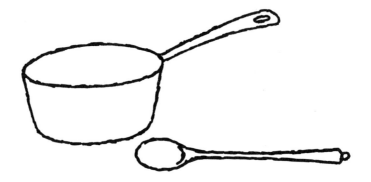

English Mixed Grill

Make expensive cuts of meat go further by boosting with less expensive foods.

(4 SERVINGS)

4 rib, loin, or shoulder lamb chops,* 1 inch thick
4 lamb kidneys, split and with the fat removed
2 tomatoes, halved
4 strips bacon (cut thick, if possible)
4 mushroom caps
melted butter
salt
pepper

Preheat broiler compartment to 350 degrees F.

Place the chops and kidneys onto a greased broiler rack, slide into the broiler, and cook for 6 minutes.

Turn the chops and kidneys and add to the broiler the tomato halves, bacon, and mushroom caps. Brush the vegetables with butter, sprinkle all with salt and pepper. Cook about 6 minutes longer or until bacon is crisp.

* Shoulder chops are the cheapest, but you might run into a sale on rib or loin chops, which are better.

Beef with Oysters

(4 SERVINGS)

1 small flank steak, thinly sliced on the bias
2 tablespoons cooking oil
1 tablespoon flour
1 teaspoon salt
1/4 teaspoon pepper
3/4 cup water or oyster liquor or bouillon
1/4 pint oysters
4 slices buttered toast with crusts trimmed

46

Pan-broil the steak slices on both sides in the cooking oil, and remove to a heated platter.

Sprinkle the flour, salt, and pepper into the pan juices, add the liquid and the oysters, and stir. Cook until the edges of the oysters curl.

To serve, place slices of steak onto toast, cover with oysters and gravy.

Pork Chops with Clams

We had this dish for the first time in a restaurant in Lisbon to the sound of the Fado singers, who sing passionately of the state of the soul, melancholy or happy.
   The Portuguese clams are smaller, but the flavor is the same.

(4 SERVINGS)

8 loin pork chops, cut thin
1/2 teaspoon salt
1/4 teaspoon pepper
1/2 can chicken broth
16 littleneck clams, well scrubbed

Brown the chops on both sides in a heavy skillet. Sprinkle with salt and pepper, add the broth and the clams in their shells (discard any that are open).

Cover and simmer gently about 20 minutes or until shells are open and chops are well done. Serve each person 2 chops and 4 clams with sauce.

Meat Extender #3: Cheese

Veal with Cheese

(4 SERVINGS)

8 thin slices of veal cut from the leg
1 egg, beaten with a little water
$1/_4$ teaspoon salt
$1/_4$ teaspoon pepper
bread crumbs
3 tablespoons olive oil mixed with 3 tablespoons of butter
$1/_4$ pound Fontina or Muenster cheese
4 thin slices prosciutto or other ham

Pound the veal and cut away the white connecting tissue, adjusting so that there are 2 thin slices per person.

Season the egg mixture with salt and pepper.

Dip the slices first into the egg, then into the crumbs, and fry quickly in the oil mixture, heated until barely smoking.

When slices are well done on one side, turn and cover with slices of cheese and prosciutto. Top with another slice of veal, cooked side down, and skewer together. When under side is brown, turn, brown the top, and serve.

Chuck and Cheese

(4 SERVINGS)

1½ **pounds chopped chuck**
4 **slices American, Muenster, or other cheese**
½ **teaspoon salt**
¼ **teaspoon pepper**
½ **cut water**

Preheat oven to 300 degrees F.

Form the chuck into 2 flat steaks, cover one with the cheese and then lay the other on top. Press together around the sides, place into a shallow pan, and brown on both sides.
Slide the pan into the oven and cook 20 minutes or until cheese has melted. Remove and cut into 4 servings.

Add the salt, pepper, and water to the pan and stir, getting the brown bits into the gravy. Spoon a little onto each serving.

Meat Extender #4: Eggs

Schnitzel à la Holstein

Veal is expensive, so to make a dish that you can afford, it is necessary to extend the meat by adding other ingredients.

(4 SERVINGS)

1 **pound veal cutlet, sliced into 4 pieces and pounded thin**
5 **eggs**
1 **tablespoon water**
bread crumbs
½ **cup cooking oil**
4 **anchovies**

Score the edges of the cutlets to prevent curling and dip them first into a beaten egg (into which water has been added), then into the crumbs.

Heat the oil to barely smoking in a heavy skillet, and brown the cutlets on both sides. Remove to a heated platter and keep warm.

Break 4 eggs into the pan and fry over low heat until done. Place an egg onto each cutlet, lay an anchovy on top, and serve.

Corned Beef (Roast Beef) Hash and Egg

This is a favorite old dish made from leftovers. It's a great way to stretch roast beef (or corned beef) and bring down the cost of the original purchase, and, with an egg on top, you need less meat beneath.

(4 SERVINGS)

**1½ cups chopped cooked beef
2 cups chopped cooked potatoes
2 tablespoons chopped onion
½ cup chopped green pepper (optional)
½ cup stock
salt
pepper
cooking oil
4 eggs**

Mix together the first seven ingredients and spread evenly over the bottom of a heavy, oiled skillet.

Cook very slowly until browned on the bottom (about ½ hour). Do not stir or turn. Fold like an omelet and slide out onto a hot platter.

Poach the eggs and set on top of hash.

Breast of Veal with Rice Stuffing

(4 SERVINGS)

1 cup cooked rice
1 small onion, chopped
1 clove garlic, minced
1/4 teaspoon pepper
1/2 teaspoon thyme
1/2 teaspoon rosemary
1 breast of veal (about 4 pounds) with a pocket cut into it
bacon fat or cooking oil

50

Preheat oven to 325 degrees F.

Mix together the rice, onion, garlic, and seasonings, and stuff into the pocket of the veal. Fasten with toothpicks or skewers.

Place into a baking dish, brush with bacon fat, cover and cook in the oven for 2½ to 3 hours.

Remove cover and continue cooking for ½ hour longer or until meat is fork-tender.

Slice between the ribs and serve hot or cold.

Baked Stuffed Pork Chops

(4 SERVINGS)

4 shoulder pork chops, 1 inch thick
2 cups dry bread crumbs
2 tablespoons chopped onions
1 teaspoon salt
pinch sage
½ cup water

Preheat oven to 350 degrees F.

Trim a small slice of fat from each of the chops. Place the chops into a hot skillet and brown on one side on top of the stove. Transfer to baking dish.

Mix together the remaining ingredients and spread onto the cooked side of the chops, topping each with a bit of the trimmed-off fat.

Cover, slide into the oven, and bake for about 1 hour. Uncover and cook 15 minutes longer or until stuffing is crisp.

PART II

Steaks and chops   53

When you think of steaks, you think first of porterhouse, sirloin, or filet mignon. You think of the expensive cuts that have become out-of-bounds on your budget—except on very special occasions.

But there are many fine cuts from the chuck, ribs, and flank that are tender enough to broil as you do the glamour cuts. And there are still other cuts, less tender but no less flavorful, that can be baked or braised.

And don't forget the possibility of marinating.

One of the most delicious steaks we have ever encountered was served to us in a tiny *taverna* on a side street in Athens within view of the Acropolis. True, the steak was cut from lamb, but what lamb! Our LAMB STEAK WITH GARLIC—as close as we could come to it after a language-barrier bout with the chef—tastes remarkably like the original (see Index).

We had exceptional steaks in Japan, cooked on the *hibachi* before us as we sat on the floor, but the Japanese use only the tenderest morsels of meat which, like the little Florentine steaks, are off-limits in this book.

For a real treat—also within your budget—try the Steak à la Deutsch or Steak Tarragon.

Pan-broiled Steak — Basic Recipe

broilable steak,* up to 1½ inches thick
salt
freshly ground pepper

Trim excess fat from the steak and score the edges to prevent curling. Wipe dry (this promotes even browning).

Preheat a heavy skillet, and drop the steak in. If steak is very lean, a little salt in the bottom of the skillet will prevent sticking.

Brown on one side. Turn, and continue cooking until blood appears on top surface. You will have a medium-rare steak. Cook longer if desired.

Remove to a heated platter or carving board and season to taste with salt and pepper.

° The following are the standard broiling steak cuts: sirloin, porterhouse, T-bone, club, Delmonico, filet mignon, and rib steak. Also broilable: top round, flank steak, shoulder steak, blade chuck (top quality only), Saratoga steak, petite (chicken) steak, boneless sirloin, barbecue steak, London broil (sirloin), skirt steak, and flanken. All of these cuts must come from high quality Choice beef or it will be necessary to marinate or tenderize before broiling.

Oven-broiled Steak — Basic Recipe

broilable steak,* more than 1½ inches thick
salt
freshly ground pepper

Preheat broiler compartment to 550 degrees F.

Trim excess fat from the steak, score the edges to prevent curling, and wipe dry.

Place on broiler rack that has been greased to prevent sticking. Slide the steak into the broiler about an inch from the heat.

Broil until top side is brown, at which time the steak should be half done. Season top side with salt and pepper, turn and brown on other side. Season again and serve.

A 2-inch steak should take about 12 minutes on each side for rare — 15 for medium.

° See note on pan-broiled steak.

Charcoal-broiled Steak — Basic Recipe

55

(4 SERVINGS)

3 pounds Choice blade chuck or London broil, 2 inches thick
1 clove garlic, crushed, mixed into
4 tablespoons melted butter (optional)
salt
freshly ground pepper

Trim excess fat from steak, cut gashes around edges to prevent curling, and blot dry with towel.

Broil about 3 minutes over white-hot charcoals as close to heat as possible. Brush with melted garlic butter. Trim and repeat on other side.

Raise grill to about 6 inches above coals and continue broiling to desired doneness. Brush occasionally with garlic butter.

Remove to a heated platter or carving board and season well with salt and pepper.

Dripping fat into charcoal fire may flare up and sear the steak. This can be prevented, if desired, by spraying with water.

Steak Arabian

(4 SERVINGS)

1/2-inch-thick strips
1/2 cup olive oil
1 large onion, sliced
2 green peppers, sliced
1 (2-ounce) can pimentos, chopped
2 1/2 pounds blade chuck steak,* boned and sliced
   diagonally into 1/2-inch-thick strips
2 cloves garlic, minced
juice of 1 lemon
salt
pepper

Place oil, onion, and peppers into a heavy skillet and cook slowly until brown. Push to side of pan.

Add the pimentos and steak slices and cook 3 minutes. Add the garlic, then the lemon juice, stirring.

Season with salt and pepper and cook 3 minutes longer, or to desired doneness.

° Only top grade USDA Choice will be tender enough for this recipe — unless the meat is tenderized (see Index).

Baked Steak

(4 SERVINGS)

2 1/2 pounds blade chuck steak
1 clove garlic, cut
salt
pepper
4 onions, sliced
1/2 lemon, sliced
1/2 cup tomato soup
2 tablespoons Worcestershire sauce
2 tablespoons melted butter

Preheat oven to 350 degrees F.

Remove the bone and excess fat from the steak, score the edges, and rub both sides with garlic, salt, and pepper.

Place into a shallow buttered pan and cover with onions and lemon slices. Pour on the tomato soup mixed with Worcestershire and butter.

Bake for about 1 hour or until meat is fork-tender. Serve from the baking dish.

Small Steaks Bayou

(4 SERVINGS)

**2 pounds steak,* ½ inch thick
cooking oil
4 potatoes, thinly sliced
water
1 medium onion, sliced
1 teaspoon salt
1 teaspoon pepper
½ teaspoon cayenne
1 teaspoon paprika
2 tablespoons butter**

In a heavy skillet cook the steaks quickly on both sides, using a little oil.

Add the potato slices and just enough water to cover. Simmer gently 15 minutes.

Add the onion slices and seasonings and cook uncovered until nearly dry. Add the butter and serve.

* Use any small, thin cuts.

Coventry Steaks

(4 SERVINGS)

8 small boneless steaks, about ¼ pound each
flour
salt
pepper
6 tablespoons oil
1 onion, chopped
2 tablespoons vinegar
1 tablespoon brown sugar
1 cup catsup
4 tablespoons Worcestershire sauce
1 cup cream

Dredge steaks with flour, season with salt and pepper. Place into a heavy skillet of preheated oil, and brown on both sides.

Add the onion, then the vinegar, brown sugar, catsup, Worcestershire, and cream.

Cook slowly for 15 minutes and serve.

Chuck-Wagon Steak Sandwiches

(4 SERVINGS)

½ cup soy sauce
½ cup water
1 clove garlic, crushed
2 onions, chopped
3 tablespoons sugar
4½ pound steaks*
1 cup sliced mushrooms
5 tablespoons butter
½ cup flour
2 teaspoons salt
½ teaspoon pepper
milk
olive oil
8 slices toasted, buttered French bread
4 slices tomatoes

Mix together the soy sauce, water, garlic, onions, and sugar, and marinate the steaks for about 1 hour at room temperature.

Sauté the mushrooms in the butter. Stir in flour, salt, and pepper, and gradually add enough milk to make a thick sauce. Keep hot.

Brush steaks with olive oil and grill over hot charcoals.

Place steaks on toasted bread, cover with tomato slices, spoon over the mushroom sauce and cover with second slice of toast.

° Any small, thin steaks will do.

Steak à la Deutsch

(4 SERVINGS)

> **2¹/₂ pounds Choice blade chuck, shoulder, or rib steak, ¹/₂ inch thick**
> **6 tablespoons butter**
> **2 medium onions, chopped**
> **4 mushrooms, sliced**
> **2 green peppers, thinly sliced**
> **2 tablespoons tomato paste**
> **2 tablespoons cream**
> **¹/₂ cup dry sherry**
> **salt**
> **pepper**
> **minced parsley**

Pan-broil the steak in a heavy buttered skillet to desired doneness and remove to a heated platter.

Into the same skillet add the onions, mushrooms, and peppers, Sauté for a few minutes.

Add the tomato paste, cream, and sherry. Simmer for a few minutes, pour the sauce over the steak, season with salt and pepper, and garnish with parsley.

Steak Diane

This is a very elegant dish calling for a club or Delmonico steak, but if you try I am sure you can find a budget cut tender enough — a rib steak, shoulder steak, or other cut from Choice chuck.

(4 SERVINGS)

2 pounds broilable steak,* 1 inch thick
6 tablespoons butter
4 tablespoons chopped green onions
2 tablespoons Worcestershire sauce
1 tablespoon dry mustard
salt
freshly ground pepper
4 tablespoons cognac or whiskey
chopped parsley

If steak contains bone, remove it. Trim off excess fat and tail (if any), and score edges.

Place steak between 2 pieces of waxed paper and pound until about ½ inch thick.

Brown quickly on both sides in a hot skillet with butter. Remove and keep hot.

To the skillet add the onions, Worcestershire, mustard, and a little salt and pepper. Simmer slowly until brown.

Return steak to skillet and cook in the sauce about 2 minutes on each side.

Heat the cognac, ignite, and pour over the steak. (If you don't happen to have brandy on hand, use Bourbon — or even gin — but be sure to warm it first or it won't ignite.)

Remove to serving platter, garnish with chopped parsley, season with salt and pepper and serve at once.

° See note on pan-broiled steak.

Flank Steak, Mustard Sauce

(4 SERVINGS)

1 large onion, chopped
4 tablespoons butter
2 pounds flank steak, sliced diagonally into ¼-
   inch-thick strips
flour
2 tablespoons vinegar
2 teaspoons dry mustard
1 teaspoon paprika
½ teaspoon thyme
1 teaspoon salt
½ teaspoon cayenne
1 cup water

In a heavy skillet brown the onion in 2 tablespoons butter. Push to side of skillet.

Dredge the steak slices with flour, add them to the pan, and brown quickly on both sides. Remove to a heated platter.

To the same skillet add 2 tablespoons butter, stir in 1 tablespoon flour, and the remaining ingredients.

Simmer for a few minutes and pour over the steak slices and serve.

Flank Steak, Butter-Gin Flambé

This is an interesting way to dress up flank steak. The gin doesn't do much in the way of adding flavor, but it sure adds to the visual enjoyment.

(4 SERVINGS)

**2 pounds flank steak
salt
freshly ground pepper
3 tablespoons butter
4 tablespoons gin**

Pan-broil the steak in a heavy skillet to desired doneness. Season well with salt and pepper and remove to a heated platter.

In the same skillet melt the butter, heat the gin, ignite and stir into the butter.

Pour over the steak and serve while still blazing. Carve the steak diagonally into thin slices.

Hawaiian Steak Barbecue

There are all kinds of interesting ways you can handle a dish like this. For example: Place a hibachi in the middle of an outdoor table, provide your guests with sharp sticks (or skewers), and let them cook their own. Make up a variety of sauces to dip into—curried mayonnaise, barbecue sauce, or use the marinade.

(4 SERVINGS)

2¹/₂ pounds chuck steak, 1¹/₂ inches thick
2 cloves garlic, crushed
2 onions, chopped
1 cup crushed pineapple or pineapple juice
1 cup soy sauce
¹/₂ cup sherry
1 teaspoon sugar
1 teaspoon powdered ginger
1 teaspoon salt

Remove the fat and bones from the steak, cut into 1¹/₂ inch cubes, and place into a shallow dish.

Mix together the remaining ingredients, pour over the steak cubes, and marinate at room temperature for about 4 hours, stirring occasionally.

Remove from marinade, place onto skewers, and grill over white-hot charcoals.

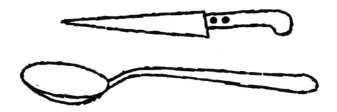

Steak à l'Oignon Belle Alliance

You'll like this dish from New Orleans. Chuck steak has a delicious flavor, and USDA Choice is usually tender enough to broil. If the cut you are cooking seems doubtful, try a little tenderizer (see Index).

(4 SERVINGS)

2½ pounds blade chuck steak, about 1 inch thick
3 tablespoons butter
4 tablespoons flour
2 cups water
6 onions, sliced
2 shallots, chopped
1 teaspoon salt
2 teaspoons freshly ground pepper
chopped parsley

Trim excess fat from the steak, score the edges to prevent curling, wipe dry, and broil on both sides to desired doneness.

Meanwhile in a skillet, melt the butter, stir in the flour and then the water. Add the onions, shallots, salt, and pepper and simmer until the onions are soft.

Pour the sauce over the steak and simmer for a few minutes. Sprinkle with parsley and serve.

Onion Steak

(4 SERVINGS)

2¹/₂ pounds Choice blade or arm chuck steak
2 medium onions, chopped
1 cup dry red wine
1 tablespoon olive oil or other cooking oil
butter
1 tablespoon Worcestershire sauce
1 cup beef stock or bouillon
salt
pepper

Place steak into a shallow dish or pan, cover with chopped onions, wine, and oil. Cover and marinate overnight in the refrigerator.

65

Drain the steak, pat dry with a napkin, and pan-broil in a heavy skillet with butter. Remove to a heated platter.

Add to the skillet 4 tablespoons of the strained wine marinade, Worcestershire, and bouillon. Simmer 2 minutes and pour over the steak. Season with salt and pepper and serve.

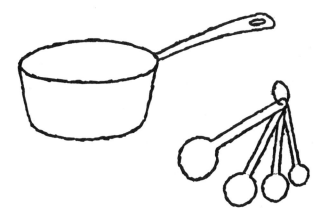

Pepper Steak, Chinese Style

(4 SERVINGS)

2½ pounds blade chuck or flank steak, about 1
   inch thick
2 tablespoons vegetable oil
1 medium onion, minced
1 clove garlic, minced
1 teaspoon salt
1 teaspoon freshly ground pepper
2 green peppers, diced
1 tablespoon Worcestershire sauce
1 cup tomatoes, drained
1 tablespoon cornstarch
2 teaspoons soy sauce
¼ cup water

Remove the bones from the steak and slice diagonally into
½-inch-thick strips.

Place oil, onion, and garlic into a heavy skillet and simmer a
few minutes.

Season the steak strips with salt and pepper and add to the
skillet.

Add the peppers and Worcestershire, cover, and cook for
½ hour.

Add tomatoes and simmer 5 minutes longer.

Combine the cornstarch, soy sauce, and water, add to the
skillet, and cook, stirring, 5 minutes.

Garlic Swiss Steak

(4 SERVINGS)

2 pounds lean steak, 1½ inches thick
salt
freshly ground pepper
½ cup flour
3 tablespoons butter
1 (12-ounce) can beer
2 tablespoons vinegar
1 teaspoon dry mustard
4 cloves garlic, chopped

Remove bone—if any—and season the steak with salt and
pepper. Cover with flour and pound thoroughly with the edge
of a plate. Turn and repeat on the other side.

Brown quickly on both sides in a heavy, buttered skillet.

Add the remaining ingredients, cover and simmer for 1 hour
or until tender.

Small Steaks, Hungarian Style

(4 SERVINGS)

2½ pounds steaks,* ½ inch thick
4 tablespoons butter
1 cup cream
3 teaspoons paprika
juice of ½ lemon
salt
pepper
cayenne

In a heavy skillet cook the steaks quickly on both sides in the
butter. Remove to a heated platter.

In the same skillet simmer the remaining ingredients gently
and pour over the steaks.

* Use any small, thin cuts.

Small Steaks with Roquefort

(4 SERVINGS)

8 tablespoons Roquefort cheese
4 tablespoons butter
½ teaspoon cayenne
1 teaspoon salt
½ teaspoon pepper
2 pounds steak,* ½ inch thick
2 tablespoons olive oil
2 tablespoons chopped parsley

Make a thick paste of the Roquefort, butter, cayenne, salt, and pepper.

In a heavy skillet quickly cook the steaks in olive oil on one side.

Remove the steaks and spread the Roquefort paste on the cooked side.

Return to the skillet, cover, and pan-broil slowly on the other side.

Garnish with parsley and serve.

* Use any small, thin cuts.

Braised Swiss Steak

(4 SERVINGS)

2 pounds lean steak, 1 inch thick
salt
pepper
½ cup flour
2 tablespoons oil
1 onion, thinly sliced
1 cup liquid (beef stock, water, or dry red wine)

Remove bone—if any—and season steak well with salt and pepper. Cover with flour and pound thoroughly with the edge of a plate. Turn and repeat on the other side.

Heat the oil in a heavy skillet and brown the steak and onions quickly on both sides.

Add the liquid, cover, and simmer about 1 hour or until tender.

Steak Stroganoff

(4 SERVINGS)

**2 pounds chuck or flank steak, sliced diagonally
into ¼-inch-thick strips
1 teaspoon salt
1 teaspoon freshly ground pepper
1 teaspoon paprika
2 tablespoons butter
1 large onion, grated
1 cup chopped mushrooms (optional)
1 tablespoon flour
1 cup beef stock or bouillon
1 cup sour cream
chopped parsley**

Tenderize steak slices (see Index) if necessary and season with salt, pepper, and paprika.

Place into a heavy skillet with 1 tablespoon butter, the onion, and the mushrooms. Broil quickly about 2 minutes.

In another skillet melt 1 tablespoon butter, stir in the flour, then the stock, and then the cream.

Add the sauce to the steak slices, stir, and simmer for about 10 minutes. Serve garnished with chopped parsley.

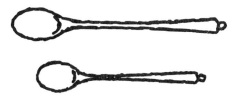

Steak au Vin

(4 SERVINGS)

2½ pounds Choice blade chuck steak
1 clove garlic, cut
¼ cup olive oil
freshly ground pepper
1 cup dry red wine
salt

Preheat broiler to 550 degrees F.

Remove excess fat from steak, score the edges, and wipe dry. Rub both sides with garlic and oil and sprinkle generously with pepper.

Place onto a greased broiler rack and broil 2 inches away from heat for 12 minutes.

Baste with half the wine, turn, and repeat on other side.

Baste with remaining wine.

Remove from oven, salt lightly on both sides, and place onto a preheated platter. Pour on the pan juices and serve.

Steak Tarragon

(4 SERVINGS)

4 ½-pound petite steaks (chicken steaks)
4 tablespoons butter
4 tablespoons chopped fresh tarragon leaves or
   1 teaspoon dried tarragon
1 cup dry red wine
2 tablespoons flour
salt
pepper

Broil the steaks quickly in 2 tablespoons butter and remove to a heated platter.

Simmer the tarragon in the wine a few minutes, using the same skillet.

In a saucepan melt 2 tablespoons butter, stir in the flour, and gradually add the tarragon wine. Stir until creamy, season, and pour over the steaks.

Lamb Steaks with Garlic

Here is a steak we had in a small restaurant in Plaka, the older section of Athens, which we think deserves to be passed along to you.

(4 SERVINGS)

2 pounds lamb steaks, 1 inch thick (good shoulder steaks will do very well)
¹⁄₂ cup dry white wine
¹⁄₂ cup olive oil
juice of 1 lemon
2 cloves garlic, crushed
1 teaspoon salt
¹⁄₂ teaspoon pepper
dash Tabasco

Place the steaks into a shallow glass or porcelain dish. Mix together all the other ingredients and pour over the steaks. Cover and allow to stand for 3 to 4 hours at room temperature.

Remove the steaks and broil over white-hot charcoals, basting with some of the marinade. Turn and repeat on the other side. The steaks should be brown and crusty on the outside and pinkish inside.

Braised Lamb Chops
with Vegetables

(4 SERVINGS)

1½ **pounds shoulder lamb chops**
1 **cup small potato balls (fresh or frozen)**
1 **cup small white onions**
1 **cup julienned carrots**
1 **tomato, peeled, seeded, and quartered**
1 **cup beef or chicken stock**
pinch marjoram
salt
pepper

Preheat oven to 350 degrees F.

Trim the bone and excess fat from the chops and put them into a casserole.

Add the remaining ingredients and the seasonings.

Cover and bake about 40 minutes or until chops are tender.

If you are in a hurry, this dish can be prepared almost as well in a pressure cooker. Brown the chops, place a rack under them, and add the remaining ingredients. Cover, bring to a 15-pound pressure, and cook for 10 minutes. Reduce the pressure, remove the cover, and serve.

Baked Paprika Pork Chops

(4 SERVINGS)

3 tablespoons flour
1 teaspoon salt
2 tablespoons paprika
2 teaspoons dry mustard
4 shoulder pork chops, 1 inch thick
3 tablespoons olive oil
2 medium onions, minced
2 tablespoons Worcestershire sauce
2 cups canned tomatoes
2 tablespoons catsup

Mix together the flour, salt, paprika, and mustard.

Dredge the chops with this mixture and fry in hot olive oil until brown, and sprinkle with onions.

Mix together the Worcestershire, tomatoes, and catsup, and pour over the chops.

Cover and cook slowly about ½ hour.

Chopped meats

*I*t will surprise no one, I am sure, to read that the most efficient and most economical way to buy meat is to buy it chopped. Bits and scraps of meat, too small to sell as steaks, chops, or roasts, but otherwise entirely acceptable as food, can be put through the grinder.

Of course, meat morsels from different sections of the animals have different flavors—and different fat content, and since most ground meat looks the same (though excess fat can easily be detected), it becomes necessary to trust your butcher's label.

Beef marked *hamburger* or simply *ground beef* is almost always a mixture of meat parts: flank, plate, shank, rib, brisket, chuck, loin, and round—and often contains added fat. Among the non-mixed meats, there is *ground sirloin*, flavorful but fat, *ground chuck*, good, lean, and usually reasonably priced, *ground round*, the most expensive.

Veal patties and *lamb patties* are almost always made from mixed parts and may vary from store to store and from day to day. Chopped pork always goes into *sausage* making.

Mix together ground beef, veal, and pork in equal proportions and you have *meat loaf.*

Ground meat, in one form or another is found all over the world. The Greeks, for example, pound ground lamb into a large loaf through which runs a spit. The loaf is then slow-cooked, turning all the while, over hot charcoals. Slices of the brown, crusty meat are then combined with slices of tomato and onion, and served with a spicy sauce on thick Greek bread. These *gyros* are encountered on the streets of Athens and throughout the country.

And what country doesn't boast of its own special kind of meat ball!

Hamburger Deluxe

(4 SERVINGS)

**1 onion, chopped
1 tablespoon chopped shallots
2 tablespoons butter
dash Tabasco
dash Worcestershire sauce
1 teaspoon dry mustard
2 teaspoons salt
½ teaspoon pepper
1½ pounds hamburger
1 egg lightly beaten
2 tablespoons sour cream**

Sauté the onions and shallots in the butter, add the Tabasco, Worcestershire, mustard, salt, and pepper. Mix together with the hamburger and egg, using the hands.

Form into loosely packed balls and drop onto kitchen table to flatten.

Pan-broil in a heavy skillet and remove to a heated platter.

Add sour cream to the pan juices, simmer a minute or so, and spoon over hamburger patties.

Chopped Steak au Poivre

(4 SERVINGS)

3 tablespoons whole black peppercorns
1½ pounds chopped steak
salt
2 tablespoons butter
dash Tabasco
1 teaspoon Worcestershire sauce
1 teaspoon lemon juice
2 tablespoons brandy or whiskey
½ cup cream
chopped parsley

Coarsely crush the peppercorns (put them in a towel and crack with the bottom of a skillet, or use a mortar and pestle).

Form the chopped steak into 4 loosely packed cakes and press crushed peppercorns into both sides.

Broil on both sides in a hot, heavy skillet until well browned on the outside and pink inside.

Season with salt and remove to a heated platter.

Into the skillet put butter, Tabasco, Worcestershire, and lemon juice.

Warm the brandy, ignite it, add to the sauce, swish it about for a minute, then add the cream.

Heat for a minute and pour over chopped steak, sprinkle with parsley and serve.

A very elegant hamburger dish!

Chopped Steak Roquefort

(4 SERVINGS)

1½ pounds chopped steak
2 tablespoons oil
¼ cup Roquefort cheese, crumbled
3 tablespoons butter
1 tablespoon dry mustard
dash Worcestershire sauce
salt
pepper

Form the chopped steak into 8 patties and brown quickly on both sides in a heavy, oiled skillet.

Mix together the Roquefort, butter, mustard, Worcestershire, salt, and pepper.

Spread Roquefort paste over the patties, cover skillet, and cook 5 minutes longer.

Salisbury Steak

(4 SERVINGS)

1½ pounds chopped steak
2 teaspoons salt
freshly ground pepper
1 cup light cream
fresh bread crumbs
1 tablespoon oil
½ cup water
2 tablespoons butter

Mix steak with seasonings and cream and form lightly into 8 patties.

Roll in bread crumbs and pan-broil in a heavy, oiled skillet. Remove to a heated platter.

To the pan juices add water, salt, and pepper, bring to a boil, scrape, add butter, and pour on steaks.

Sloppy Joe Sandwiches

(4 SERVINGS)

1/4 cup chopped onions (frozen or fresh)
1/2 cup chopped green peppers
2 tablespoons oil
1 tomato, peeled, seeded, and chopped
1 teaspoon paprika
dash Worcestershire sauce
1/4 teaspoon cayenne
1 teaspoon salt
1 1/2 pounds hamburger
8 hamburger rolls

79

Sauté the onions and peppers in a heavy oiled skillet until browned.

Add the next six ingredients (including the loose hamburger), cover, and cook over low heat 15 minutes, stirring frequently.

Spoon onto toasted hamburger rolls.

Danish Meat Balls

(4 SERVINGS)

1/2 pound hamburger, ground twice
1/2 pound lean pork, ground twice*
1/2 cup flour
1 cup milk
1 teaspoon salt
1/2 teaspoon pepper
4 tablespoons butter

Mix the 2 meats together thoroughly.

Mix the flour, milk, and seasonings together.

Combine the two mixtures and beat until light and fluffy.

Form into balls about 1 1/2 inches in diameter and sauté in butter until golden (about 15 minutes).

* Some states do not allow butchers to grind pork. You might have to grind it yourself.

German Meat Balls

½ pound hamburger
½ pound veal
1 cup cooked riced potatoes
1 tablespoon chopped canned anchovies
2 tablespoons chopped onion
1 teaspoon salt
½ teaspoon pepper
flour
1 cup chopped onions
2 tablespoons butter
2 tablespoons flour
½ teaspoon salt
1 tablespoon vinegar
2 cups water

Mix the hamburger, veal, potatoes, anchovies, onion, and seasonings together. Form into balls 1½ inches in diameter, roll in flour, and set aside.

Meanwhile sauté a cup of chopped onions in 2 tablespoons butter, add flour, salt, vinegar, and water. Cook 5 minutes, then add the meat balls and cook 15 minutes longer.

Hungarian Meat Balls

(4 SERVINGS)

1 pound hamburger, ground twice
1 clove garlic, crushed
½ cup dry bread crumbs
2 tablespoons paprika
1 teaspoon salt
1 egg, slightly beaten
¼ cup milk
butter
½ cup canned chopped mushrooms
2 tablespoons flour
2 cups sour cream
2 tablespoons chopped parsley

Mix the hamburger, garlic, bread crumbs, paprika, salt, egg, and milk together and form into balls 1½ inches in diameter.

Sauté in butter until golden (about 15 minutes) and remove to a heated platter.

Meanwhile combine mushrooms, flour, and sour cream. Cook-stir until smooth and creamy (about 5 minutes).

Pour the sauce over the meat balls and serve garnished with parsley.

Indian Meat Balls

(4 SERVINGS)

1 pound hamburger
½ cup tomato paste
½ cup dry bread crumbs
½ teaspoon salt
1½ teaspoon curry powder
2 tablespoons oil
1 cup beef bouillon
2 tablespoons chopped onion
½ cup seedless raisins
pinch ginger
1 teaspoon salt
1 tablespoon flour
½ cup water

Mix the hamburger, tomato paste, bread crumbs, salt, and ½ teaspoon curry powder together. Form into balls 1½ inches in diameter.

Sauté in oil until brown (about 6 minutes) and set aside.

To the skillet juices stir in the bouillon, onion, raisins, 1 teaspoon curry powder, ginger, and salt. Simmer 5 minutes, then thicken with 1 tablespoon flour mixed with ½ cup water.

Return the meat balls to the skillet and simmer 5 minutes longer. Serve with rice.

Italian Meat Balls

(4 SERVINGS)

1 pound hamburger
1 clove garlic, crushed
½ teaspoon orégano
1 teaspoon salt
½ teaspoon pepper
1 egg, slightly beaten
½ cup dry bread crumbs
½ cup grated Parmesan cheese
2 tablespoons olive oil

82

Mix the hamburger, garlic, seasonings, and egg together. Form into balls 1½ inches in diameter, roll in bread crumbs and cheese.

Sauté in hot oil until golden (about 10 minutes).

Serve with spaghetti.

Mexican Meat Balls

(4 SERVINGS)

½ pound hamburger
½ pound ground lean pork*
1 onion, chopped
1 teaspoon salt
½ teaspoon pepper
½ cup dry bread crumbs
2 tablespoons olive oil
1 clove garlic, crushed
1 onion, chopped
½ cup chopped green pepper
1 teaspoon chili powder
½ cup tomato paste
1 cup water

Mix the hamburger, pork, onion, salt, and pepper together. Form into balls 1½ inches in diameter and roll in bread crumbs.

Sauté in hot oil until golden (about 10 minutes) and remove to a heated platter.

To the skillet juices add the garlic, onion, green pepper, chili powder, tomato paste, and water. Cook-stir for 10 minutes and pour over the meat balls.

° Some states do not allow butchers to grind pork. You might have to grind it yourself.

Swedish Meat Balls

(4 SERVINGS)

½ pound hamburger, ground twice
½ pound pork, ground twice*
½ cup finely chopped onion
1 teaspoon salt
½ teaspoon pepper
pinch allspice
1 egg, slightly beaten and mixed with 1 cup milk
2 cups bread crumbs
2 tablespoons fat
½ can beef bouillon

Mix the hamburger, pork, onion, and seasonings together, form into balls about 1 inch in diameter. Soak in the egg-milk mixture for 1 minute or so.

Roll in bread crumbs and brown in hot fat about 5 minutes or until browned. Remove to a heated platter.

Add the beef bouillon to the pan juices. Stir and pour over the meat balls.

° Some states do not allow butchers to grind pork. You might have to grind it yourself.

Chili con Carne

(4 SERVINGS)

2 onions, chopped
1 clove garlic, crushed
2 tablespoons olive oil
1½ pounds beef, cubed or chopped
8 dried chili peppers (if you can find them)
2 tablespoons chili powder (4, if you like it hot)
1 teaspoon orégano
1 teaspoon cumin seed, crushed
1 teaspoon salt
2 cups beef bouillon

In a large heavy skillet sauté the onions and garlic in the oil for a minute or so, add the beef and brown, stirring.

Remove the stems, seeds, and skins from the chilies (to do this boil the chilies for about 20 minutes). Add the chilies to the meat along with the seasonings and bouillon.

Cook until the meat is tender and the flavors are well blended.

Serve in a bowl with Mexican pink beans (that have been soaked overnight and boiled until tender) or with canned kidney beans.

Meat Loaf

You can do almost anything with meat loaf. The meat combinations may be varied or the loaf may be made with beef, veal, or lamb alone. Add grated cheese for additional flavor — or chopped celery — or chopped olives. Vary the seasoning: add a pinch of thyme or basil. Spice it up with Worcestershire sauce, chile sauce, catsup, or Tabasco.

(4 SERVINGS)

½ **pound ground beef**
½ **pound ground veal**
½ **pound ground pork***
1 egg, slightly beaten
1 cup soft bread crumbs or 3 slices stale bread, wet and crumbled
½ **cup water or milk**
2 tablespoons finely chopped onion
2 teaspoons salt
½ **teaspoon pepper**
3 strips bacon
tomato or mushroom sauce (see Index)

Preheat oven to 350 degrees F.

Mix together the ground meats, egg, bread crumbs, milk, onion, and seasonings.

Form into a loaf and place into a greased pan.

Lay the bacon strips across the top, place into the oven, and bake for about 1 hour.

Serve as is, or with tomato or mushroom sauce.

° Some states do not allow butchers to grind pork. You might have to grind it yourself.

Shepherd's Pie

This has long been a popular way to use leftover cooked beef or lamb.

(4 SERVINGS)

3 cups chopped leftover lamb or beef
1 onion, finely chopped
1 green pepper, chopped
leftover gravy or stock
salt
pepper
mashed potatoes

Preheat oven to 400 degrees F.

Put chopped meat, onion, and pepper into a baking dish, add the gravy, season with salt and pepper, and cover with a thin layer of mashed potatoes.

Bake in the oven until well heated and the potatoes are browned.

Savory Lamb Patties

(4 SERVINGS)

1 pound ground lamb
1 teaspoon salt
$\frac{1}{2}$ teaspoon butter
1 egg
$\frac{1}{2}$ cup chili sauce
1 cup bread crumbs
cooking oil
tomato sauce (see Index)

Mix all the ingredients together and form into flat patties.

Brown quickly on both sides in a hot, oiled skillet. Lower heat, cover, and cook 20 minutes longer.

Serve with tomato sauce.

Ham Loaf

Here's a good way to use up leftover cooked ham — and bring down the cost of your original investment.

(4 SERVINGS)

3 cups ground cooked ham
¼ teaspoon salt
¼ teaspoon pepper
½ teaspoon dry mustard
1 cup fresh bread crumbs
½ cup milk
2 eggs, beaten
2 slices bacon

Preheat oven to 350 degrees F.

Mix together the ham, seasonings, bread crumbs, milk, and egg. Shape into a loaf.

Place the loaf into a shallow baking pan, cover with the bacon strips, and bake about 1 hour.

Stewing meats 89

Some of the greatest and most hearty dishes are made from some of the most unglamorous cuts of meat—cubes of beef, veal, and lamb—taken from the part of the animal that is most active and therefore least tender. They are often grainy in texture and sometimes, but not always, contain bits of bone.

Stewing meats cooked with care and seasoned with imagination can produce some of the most delicious dishes—international favorites such as Boeuf Bourguigonne, Blanquette de Veau, Hungarian Goulash, Irish Stew, Veal Paprika, to name a few. It is in the preparation of such dishes that the cook has his greatest opportunity to be really creative.

Boeuf Bourguignonne and goulash are well known to all, but how about Greek Fricassee? Try this fantastic stew we discovered in Athens.

Old-fashioned Beef Stew

(4 SERVINGS)

> 2 pounds lean, boneless, stewing beef (chuck or shin), cut into 1½-inch cubes
> 2 teaspoons salt
> 1 teaspoon pepper
> flour
> 2 tablespoons cooking oil or bacon fat
> 1 onion, sliced
> 1 clove garlic (optional)
> pinch thyme
> boiling water or beef stock or dry red wine

Season the meat cubes with salt and pepper and dredge with flour.

Heat the cooking oil in a heavy skillet and brown the meat cubes on all sides.

Add the onion, and garlic, and a pinch of thyme. Cover with boiling water, stock, or red wine (or a combination of them). Cover and simmer slowly for about 2 hours or until meat is fork-tender.

Convert this basic stew into a beef-vegetable stew by adding 1 large sliced carrot, 2 cubed potatoes, and any other vegetable you wish (peas, green beans, mushrooms, turnips). Vegetables should be added after the stew has cooked 1½ hours.

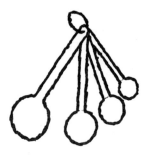

Oxtail Ragout

Oxtail is largely bone but the meat has a fine flavor and is one of those dishes that gains by reheating.

(4 SERVINGS)

2 pounds oxtail, disjointed
flour
2 tablespoons cooking oil
2 onions, sliced
2 teaspoons salt
½ teaspoon pepper
½ bay leaf
1 cup bouillon or stock
2 cups water
2 carrots, sliced
1 small turnip, cubed
1 cup diced celery
1 green pepper, chopped

Wash and dry the oxtail, dredge with flour, and brown in hot cooking oil together with the onions, using a heavy skillet.

Add the salt, pepper, bay leaf, bouillon, and water. Cover and simmer about 3 hours or until meat is tender.

Add the vegetables and simmer ½ hour longer or until vegetables are cooked.

Remove meat and vegetables to warm serving dish, thicken the broth (if necessary) with a water-flow mixture, and check seasoning.

Pour the sauce over the meat and vegetables and serve.

Boeuf à la Bourguignonne

In Burgundy this famous dish is cooked 6 hours in a slow oven. Try cooking it this way if you have the time.

(4 SERVINGS)

4 ounces salt pork, cubed, or 6 slices bacon
8 small white onions
2 pounds beef (chuck or shin), cut into 1½-inch cubes
salt
pepper
flour
1 clove garlic, crushed
4 shallots, chopped
½ teaspoon thyme
½ bay leaf
1½ cups water
1½ cups burgundy or other dry red wine
½ cup sliced mushrooms
2 ounces brandy (optional)

Put the salt pork (or bacon) into a heavy skillet and cook until brown and crisp. Remove and set aside.

Add the onions to the skillet, brown, remove, and set aside.

Season the meat cubes with salt and pepper, dredge them with flour, and brown well in the skillet.

Add the garlic, shallots, thyme, bay leaf, and liquid.

Cover and simmer 3 hours or until beef is fork-tender. Add more liquid, if necessary.

Return the salt pork and onions to the skillet, and add the mushrooms. Cook 15 minutes longer and just before serving flambé the brandy and add to the stew.

Hungarian Goulash

You can make goulash with either beef or veal—or with a combination of the two. Always add the paprika to the fat (never to the liquid) or it will lose its bright color. And don't use pepper with paprika or you'll ruin its flavor.

(4 SERVINGS)

½ cup cubed salt pork or 2 strips bacon
2 pounds lean, boneless stewing beef (chuck or
**   shin), cut into 1½-inch cubes**
3 medium onions, chopped
2 tablespoons flour
2 tablespoons paprika
1 clove garlic, crushed
2 teaspoons salt
2 cups boiling water or stock
2 cups dry red wine

Cook the salt pork in a heavy skillet until browned, and set aside.

Add the beef cubes and onions to the skillet and brown well.

Stir in the flour, paprika, garlic, and salt.

Add the liquid, cover, and simmer about 2 hours or until meat is tender.

Check the seasoning and sauce—it should be dark and thick. Add the salt pork cubes and serve.

Blanquette of Veal

This is a very elegant and rich dish—can be made with lamb as well if most of the fat is trimmed away. The meat—veal or lamb—is never browned.

(4 SERVINGS)

2 pounds boneless stewing veal (shoulder or breast) cut into 1½-inch cubes
water
1 large onion
2 teaspoons salt
6 peppercorns
½ bay leaf
pinch thyme
clove garlic
2 sprigs parsley
8 small white onions, peeled
2 carrots, julienned
2 tablespoons flour
2 tablespoons butter
2 egg yolks beaten with the juice of 1 lemon
few grains nutmeg

Parboil the meat for 5 minutes in a saucepan of water. Drain.

Add to the saucepan the onion, salt, peppercorns, bay leaf, thyme, garlic, parsley, and enough water to cover. Simmer, covered, for 1 hour.

Add the onions and carrots. Cover and simmer ½ hour longer or until meat is fork-tender.

Remove meat, onions, and carrots to a heated serving dish. Keep hot.

Strain the stock and reduce to almost half.

Blend the flour and butter, add to the broth, bring to a boil, and cook for 1 minute. Stir the egg yolk with lemon into a little of the broth. Add to pan until sauce thickens. Do not boil. Season with a few grains nutmeg. Pour sauce over meat and serve.

Fricassee of Veal (or Lamb)

(4 SERVINGS)

3 pounds stewing veal or lamb (2 pounds if bone-less), cut into 1½-inch cubes
2 teaspoons salt
1 teaspoon pepper
flour
cooking oil
4 cups boiling water
½ bay leaf
1 onion, chopped
1 carrot, sliced
4 sprigs parsley
2 cups other vegetables such as peas, green beans, diced turnip, diced celery (optional)

Remove excess fat from the meat and discard it.

Season the meat cubes with salt and pepper, dredge with flour, and brown well in a heavy skillet with a little hot cooking oil.

Add 4 cups boiling water, cover, and simmer for 1½ hours.

Add the bay leaf, onion, carrot, parsley, and any other vegetables you might wish. Thicken sauce, if necessary with a flour and water mixture.

Cover and simmer ½ hour longer.

Veal Paprika

(4 SERVINGS)

2 tablespoons cooking oil
2 pounds veal shoulder, cut into 1-inch cubes
2 medium onions, chopped
1/2 clove garlic, crushed
1/2 cup chopped green pepper
1 cup canned tomato
1 teaspoon salt
1 tablespoon paprika (or more, to taste)
1 cup water

Heat oil in a heavy skillet. Add the meat, onions, garlic, and pepper, and cook for about 10 minutes, stirring.

Add paprika and then the tomato, salt, and water. Cover and continue cooking about 1 hour or until meat is fork-tender. Add more water if necessary.

Irish Lamb Stew

Real Irish stew needs no flour. It thickens itself as the thinly sliced potatoes dissolve. Real Irish stew contains no vegetables except potatoes and onions, but if you wish you can add carrots, turnips, beans, and almost anything else you might have on hand. Vegetables should go into the stew along with the whole potatoes.

(6 SERVINGS)

3 pounds stewing lamb (2 pounds if boneless),
  cut into 1 1/2-inch cubes
4 medium potatoes, peeled and sliced thinly
4 onions, sliced
pinch thyme
2 teaspoons salt
1 teaspoon pepper
2 cups water
4 medium potatoes, peeled but left whole

Put everything except the whole potatoes into a pot, cover, and simmer for 1½ hours. Add more water if necessary.

Add the whole potatoes, cover, and cook 1 hour longer. Check seasoning and serve in bowls.

Greek Fricassee

Here is a most delicious and unusual dish we found in Athens. It was served to us in a relatively expensive restaurant, but the dish is well qualified to be included in a book of budget recipes and we heartily urge you to try it.

(6 SERVINGS)

3 pounds stewing lamb
3 tablespoons olive oil
1 bunch spring onions with green parts included, chopped
1 head romaine lettuce or 2 endives, shredded
2 tablespoons chopped dill (1 tablespoon dried)
1 teaspoon chopped fresh mint (½ teaspoon dried)
1 teaspoon salt
½ teaspoon pepper
water
2 tablespoons butter
2 tablespoons flour
juice of 1 lemon
2 eggs, well beaten

Using a heavy skillet sauté the meat in the oil for 20 minutes, turning to brown on all sides. Add the onions, lettuce, herbs, and seasonings, cover with water, and simmer slowly about 1½ hours or until meat is tender.

While the fricassee is cooking, prepare egg-lemon sauce (the Greeks call it *avgolemono saltsa*) in the following manner: Make a roux with the butter and flour, cook for a few minutes, and stir in 2 cups of the broth from the stew until the sauce becomes smooth. Beat the lemon juice into the egg, add 2 teaspoons cold water, then slowly pour in the hot stock. Do not boil or sauce will curdle. Add the sauce to the fricassee and serve hot.

Sweet and Sour Pork (or Spareribs)

(4 SERVINGS)

1 green pepper, cut into 1-inch cubes
water
1 egg
2 tablespoons flour
$\frac{1}{2}$ teaspoon salt
$\frac{1}{8}$ teaspoon pepper
1 pound boneless pork shoulder, cut into 1-inch
    cubes or 3 pounds lean pork spareribs, cut into
    serving pieces
$\frac{1}{2}$ cup cooking oil
1 cup chicken bouillon
$\frac{1}{2}$ cup canned pineapple chunks
2 tablespoons cornstarch
2 tablespoons soy sauce
$\frac{1}{4}$ cup sugar
$\frac{1}{4}$ cup vinegar

Simmer the peppers in a little water for a couple of minutes and drain.

Beat together the egg, flour, and seasonings, and dip the pork cubes into this batter.

Heat the oil in a heavy skillet and brown the pork cubes on all sides. Remove to a heated serving dish.

Pour off the oil and add the bouillon, the green pepper, and pineapple chunks. Cover and simmer about 10 minutes.

Stir in the remaining ingredients and simmer until the mixture is clear (about 3 minutes); pour it over the pork and serve.

Mexican Pork Stew

(4 SERVINGS)

1½ pounds pork shoulder, cut into 1-inch cubes
2 medium onions, sliced
2 tablespoons cooking oil
2 cups canned tomatoes
¼ cup chopped green pepper
¼ cup chopped celery
1 tablespoon chili powder
1 teaspoon salt
1 tablespoon flour mixed with 2 tablespoons water

Remove excess fat from meat.

Heat the cooking oil in a heavy skillet and add the pork and onions. Brown well.

Add all remaining ingredients, cover, and simmer 1 hour.

Roasts, pot roasts,   *101*
and briskets

*T*hese are the chunky cuts. They come roughly in two grades—first class: beef rib roast, beef sirloin, leg of veal, leg of lamb, loin of pork and ham; and economy class: beef chuck roast, California roast, London broil, pot roast, fresh brisket of beef, corned beef, shoulder of veal, arm or blade roast of veal, rolled shoulder of lamb, shoulder of pork.

Both grades of meat are wonderfully easy to cook—if you have the time. First-class roasts are merely inserted into a hot oven. Economy cuts are cooked in liquid.

I remember a dish we had in Rome called *bollito misto*, actually a very common dish in Italy, that consisted of a wagon of boiled meats. The waiter served us slices of the meats we selected.

Pot Roast of Beef

(8 SERVINGS)

2 tablespoons flour
1 teaspoon salt
¹/₂ teaspoon pepper
¹/₂ teaspoon sugar
1 tablespoon cooking oil
4 pounds beef chuck roast or California roast, trimmed, rolled, and tied
1 onion, sliced
1 cup water or tomato juice

Mix together the flour, salt, pepper, and sugar (to help browning), and rub into the surface of the meat.

Heat the oil in a heavy pot and brown the roast on all sides with the onion for ¹/₂ hour or more.

Add the liquid, cover, and cook slowly 3 to 4 hours or until meat is fork-tender. (You might have to add a little more liquid, as it cooks away.)

Remove the meat, skim any fat that may have accumulated, pour the thickened gravy over the pot roast, and serve.

Beef à la Mode

This is a glorified version of pot roast.

(8 SERVINGS)

4 pounds beef chuck roast or California roast, trimmed, rolled, and tied
1 tablespoon salt
¹/₂ teaspoon pepper
3 onions, sliced
3 carrots, sliced
3 sprigs parsley
2 bay leaves
1 cup dry red wine
water
1 tablespoon oil

Place the meat into a glass or pottery bowl, add all the remaining ingredients and enough water to cover. Cover the bowl and let stand overnight.

Drain off the marinade and save.

Dry the meat with a paper towel. Heat oil in a heavy pot and brown the meat on all sides. Add the marinade, cover, and cook slowly 3 to 4 hours or until meat is fork-tender.

Skim off any fat that may have accumulated, and serve the beef in the thickened gravy.

Can be served cold, as well.

Sauerbraten 103

(8 SERVINGS)

> 4 pounds beef chuck roast or California roast, trimmed, rolled, and tied
> 1 teaspoon salt
> freshly ground pepper
> 1 tablespoon brown sugar
> 2 onions, sliced
> 2 bay leaves
> 1 cup dry red wine (or wine vinegar)
> water
> 2 tablespoons flour
> 2 tablespoons oil
> ½ cup sour cream

Place the beef into a glass or pottery bowl, sprinkle with salt, pepper, and brown sugar, and add the onions and bay leaves. Add the wine or vinegar and enough water to cover the meat. Cover the bowl and let stand a day or two.

Drain off the marinade and save.

Dry the meat with a paper towel and dredge with flour.

Heat the oil in a heavy pot and brown the meat on all sides with the onions. Add the marinade, cover, and cook slowly 3 to 4 hours or until meat is fork-tender.

Remove the meat. Strain the sauce, add the sour cream, and heat. Do not boil. Place meat into the sauce and serve.

Corned Beef and Cabbage

(8 SERVINGS)

4 pounds lean corned beef (brisket is best)
water
1 small cabbage, quartered and cored

Wash beef under running water to remove brine. Place into a heavy pot, cover with cold water, bring slowly to a boil. After 5 minutes skim the scum, cover the pot, and simmer 3 to 4 hours or until meat is tender.

Remove 2 cups of the liquid to another pot, add the cabbage, and cook about 15 minutes or until tender. Serve with the corned beef.

New England Boiled Dinner

(8 SERVINGS)

4 pounds lean corned beef (preferably brisket)
water
4 medium potatoes, peeled and halved
8 small carrots
2 medium turnips, peeled and quartered
8 small white onions

Wash the beef under running water, place into a large pot, cover with cold water, and bring slowly to a boil. After 5 minutes skim the scum, cover the pot, and simmer 3 hours.

Add the vegetables, cover, and simmer 1 hour longer or until everything is nice and tender but not mushy.

Roast Shoulder of Veal

(6 SERVINGS)

4 pounds shoulder of veal, boned and tied
1 clove garlic, cut
flour
salt
pepper
fat salt pork

Preheat oven to 325 degrees F.

Wipe the meat dry with a towel, rub well with garlic, and sprinkle with a little flour, salt, and pepper.

Place roast onto the rack of a roasting pan and cover with strips of salt pork. Slide into the oven and roast about 2½ hours or until meat is tender. Veal should be well done. A meat thermometer will read 180 degrees when the veal is well done.

Serve with the pan juices, or make a gravy by stirring in a tablespoon of flour and thinning with milk or water.

For an unusual version of the above recipe, cut gashes into the meat before cooking and squeeze a little anchovy paste into them.

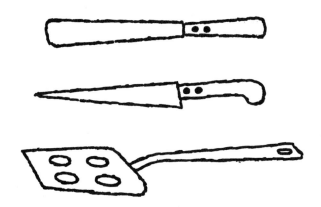

Roast Shoulder of Lamb

(4 SERVINGS)

4 pounds shoulder of lamb, boned and tied
1 clove garlic, thinly sliced
seasoning as preferred: ginger, thyme, marjo-
ram, or caraway seed

Preheat oven to 325 degrees F.

Wipe the lamb dry with a towel, cut shallow gashes into the meat and insert slivers of garlic, season as desired, place onto the rack of a roasting pan, and slide into the oven.

Roast 1½ hours if you like pink lamb, 2½ for well done. A meat thermometer will read 170 degrees for pink, 175 degrees for medium, and 180 degrees for well done.

Serve with pan juices, or make a gravy by stirring in a table-spoon of flour, a little salt and pepper, and thinning with milk or water.

Roast Loin (or Shoulder) of Pork

(6 SERVINGS)

5 pounds loin of pork with backbone separated
and ribs sawed through or 4 pounds shoulder
boned and tied

Preheat oven to 350 degrees F.

Place roast fat side up, onto rack of a shallow roasting pan, slide into the oven, and cook 2½ to 3 hours or until pork is well done. A meat thermometer should read 185 degrees.

Serve with pan juices and fried apples, applesauce, or glazed pineapple. Or make a gravy by stirring in a tablespoon of flour, a little salt and pepper, and thinning with water or milk.

Smoked Pork Tenderloin

(4 TO 6 SERVINGS)

2 pounds pork butt or daisy ham
water
2 tablespoons brown sugar
1 tablespoon flour
1 tablespoon vinegar

Remove the paper wrapping, and the "stocking" from the pork butt and put it in water to cover over medium heat until it comes to a boil. Lower the heat to simmer and cook 35 minutes to the pound.

Preheat oven to 350 degrees F.

Remove the pork butt from the water. (Save the water for baked beans or split pea soup.) Put the pork butt in a small roasting pan. Mix the brown sugar, the flour, the vinegar and spread the mixture over the pork butt. Put it in the oven for 25 to 30 minutes.

Some pork butts can be cooked entirely in the oven. The imprint on the wrapping will say whether or not this can be done.

Baked Picnic Ham

(6 TO 8 SERVINGS)

6 pounds picnic ham
4 tablespoons brown sugar
whole cloves

Preheat oven to 350 degrees F.

Cook tenderized hams 20 to 25 minutes per pound, ordinary hams 35 minutes per pound, or both to 170 degrees F. on a meat thermometer. (Read directions on the ham wrapper.) Count on 4 pounds of meat and 2 pounds of bones.

Put the ham in an open roasting pan fat side up and cover with aluminum foil and cook 1½ hours.

Remove the ham from the oven, remove the foil, remove the skin, if any, and score the fat crosswise diamond fashion. Put the cloves in the fat where the scorings cross. Sift the brown sugar evenly over all, and brown in the oven ½ hour.

Baked Ham with Pineapple

(4 SERVINGS)

1½ pounds ham, sliced 1 inch thick
prepared mustard (preferably Dijon)
¼ cup brown sugar
½ cup pineapple syrup (from canned pineapples)
6 slices pineapple

Preheat the oven to 350 degrees F.

Slash the edges of the ham slice to prevent curling and place into a baking dish. Spread with mustard and brown sugar, and pour on the syrup.

Place into the oven and bake about 1 hour.

Place the pineapple slices on top and cook 15 minutes longer or until ham is tender and pineapple is browned. Baste frequently.

You wouldn't generally rate a slice of ham as an inexpensive cut of meat, but there is little bone and no waste, so a little can go a long way. An interesting variation of the above recipe is to substitute slices of a peeled and cored apple for the pineapple.

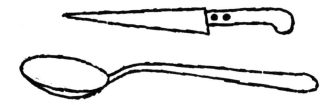

Ribs, breasts, and shanks   *111*

*T*hese cuts of meat are characterized by a large content of bone and a large measure of succulence. In the market the price tag is correspondingly low, but one would be advised to examine carefully how much bone is being bought. Bone-in meats are not always a bargain.

In general, ribs, breasts, and shanks will require slow cooking (braising or baking) to break down the tissue ever-present in such cuts. But the reward in this eating is well worth the trouble in the cooking.

Braised Short Ribs of Beef

(4 SERVINGS)

4 pounds beef short ribs (the meatier the better)
1 onion, sliced (optional)
salt
pepper

Place the ribs into a heavy skillet and brown well on all sides.

Pour off the accumulated fat, place the onions on top of the ribs, cover the skillet, and cook slowly for about 1½ hours or until fork-tender.

Season with salt and pepper and serve.

Short ribs can also be roasted without embellishment in a preheated 325-degree oven for 2 hours.

Baked Breast of Veal with Vegetables

(4 SERVINGS)

¼ pound salt pork, diced
1 breast of veal (about 4 pounds)
6 small carrots
6 small onions, peeled
6 small potatoes, peeled
1 small rutabaga, peeled and cubed
1 clove garlic, peeled
½ teaspoon salt
¼ teaspoon pepper
½ cup dry white wine
1 cup water
few sprigs parsley, chopped

Preheat oven to 325 degrees F.

Using a heavy skillet render the salt pork, remove, and set aside.

Brown the veal breast on both sides in the pork fat and set aside.

Add the carrots, onions, potatoes, rutabaga, and garlic to the skillet and brown.

Sprinkle the pork bits over the vegetables, place the breast on top outside up, season with salt and pepper, add the liquid, cover, and bake for 2½ hours or until meat is tender.

Garnish with parsley and serve.

113

Baked Breast of Lamb

(4 SERVINGS)

4 pounds breast of lamb
salt
pepper

Preheat oven to 350 degrees F.

Dry the meat with a paper towel, season with salt and pepper, and place into the rack of a baking pan.

Bake uncovered about 2 hours or until meat is fork-tender.

For a variation of the above follow the recipe for Stuffed Breast of Veal (see Index) leaving out the salt pork and gravy.

Braised Lamb Riblets

(4 SERVINGS)

2 medium onions, chopped
2 tablespoons olive oil
2 pounds lamb riblets
2 tablespoons vinegar
2 tablespoons lemon juice
2 tablespoons brown sugar
1/4 cup chili sauce
1/4 cup tomato catsup
1/2 cup dry red wine
pinch rosemary
1/2 teaspoon salt
freshly ground pepper

114

Using a heavy skillet, sauté the onions in the olive oil until tender. Do not brown. Strain off the onion and discard.

Cut the riblets into serving pieces, remove excess fat, and brown on all sides in the oil.

Add all the remaining ingredients, cover and simmer about 1 hour or until riblets are tender.

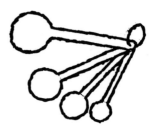

Barbecued Lamb Ribs
Chinese Style

There was a time long, long ago — it seems — when pork spare-ribs were regarded as economy fare. No longer! But even these days you can enjoy a meal of ribs and still meet last month's mortgage payment if the ribs you serve come from lamb. The recipe that follows may be used for a cookout main dish, or for party appetizers served with drinks.

(4 SERVINGS)

3 pounds breast of young lamb, cut into ribs
3 tablespoons heavy soy sauce
5 tablespoons light soy sauce
2 tablespoons sugar
2 tablespoons honey
3 tablespoons applesauce or crushed pineapple (pineapple juice will do)
3 tablespoons rice wine (gin will do nicely)
2 cloves garlic, crushed
1 teaspoon salt

Trim excess fat from ribs and place them into a shallow dish.

Mix together the remaining ingredients, pour over the ribs, cover, and allow to stand for about 2 hours, occasionally stirring.

Grill over white-hot charcoals until crusty on the outside and pink inside. Brush from time to time with some of the marinade. Flames from dripping fat may be extinguished, if you wish, by spraying with water.

Barbecued Lamb Shanks

(4 SERVINGS)

4 lamb shanks (about 6 pounds)
2 tablespoons cooking oil
2 onions, sliced
1 cup water
1 cup catsup
2 tablespoons Worcestershire sauce
½ cup vinegar
3 tablespoons brown sugar
1 teaspoon dry mustard
2 teaspoons salt
1 teaspoon pepper

Using a heavy skillet, brown the shanks in the cooking oil. Add the remaining ingredients, cover, and cook for about 2 hours or until tender, spooning the sauce over the meat several times.

Remove the cover and cook 15 minutes longer.
This dish can be made with a veal shank cut into 4 portions.

Braised Lamb Shanks

(4 SERVINGS)

4 lamb shanks (about 6 pounds)
flour
salt
pepper
2 tablespoons cooking oil
1 bay leaf
1 onion sliced
boiling water

Dredge the shanks in flour, season with salt and pepper, and brown well in cooking oil, using a heavy skillet.

Add the bay leaf, onion, and just enough boiling water to cover the meat.

Reduce the heat, cover the skillet, and simmer slowly for about 2 hours or until tender.

If you wish, add a cup each of diced carrots, diced potatoes, and diced celery ½ hour before the meat is done.

This dish can be made with a veal shank cut into 4 portions.

Barbecued Pork Spareribs

Pork spareribs are not exactly budget fare. True, they don't cost very much, but there's not much meat on them, either. Loin ribs are meatier than regular ribs, but they are more expensive. So if you are budget-minded, watch out for this dish.

(4 SERVINGS)

> **4 pounds spareribs (or 3 pounds of loin ribs), cut into 2-rib pieces**
> **salt**
> **pepper**
> **chopped onion**
> **barbecue sauce (see Index)**

Preheat oven to 350 degrees F.

Place the ribs into a shallow baking pan, season with salt and pepper, and top each with a little chopped onion.

Bake for 1½ hours, basting occasionally with barbecue sauce and turning from time to time.

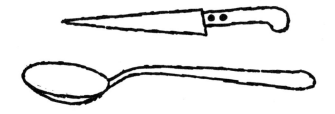

Pork Spareribs and Sauerkraut

(4 SERVINGS)

3 pounds spareribs, cut into serving pieces
1 quart fresh sauerkraut
1 teaspoon salt
water

Place the spareribs and sauerkraut into a large pot, season with salt, and cover with water.

Cover the pot and simmer for 1½ hours. Drain and serve.

Baked Stuffed Pork Spareribs

Add a little stuffing to meat and you make it go farther.

(4 SERVINGS)

1 pair spareribs, cracked (about 3 pounds)
2 cups bread or New England or sausage stuff-
ing (see Index)

Preheat oven to 350 degrees F.

Place half the ribs on the rack of a baking pan and cover with stuffing. Cover with the other ribs and bake about 1½ hours or until tender, basting from time to time.

Ham Shank and Beans

(6 SERVINGS)

1 ham shank
water
2 cups navy beans, soaked overnight
2 onions, sliced
¼ cup black molasses
2 teaspoons dry mustard

Place ham shank into a pot, cover with water, bring to a boil, then simmer for 3 hours or until meat separates from bone.

Discard the bone, dice the ham, and return it to the broth.

119

Add the remaining ingredients, cover, and simmer for about 3 more hours.

Pork hocks, knuckles, *feet, and trotters*

*T*hese meats are high in flavor and low in cost. All are related, constituting as they do the extremities of the hog or pig, all contain a great deal of bone and fat, and all require a great deal of cooking.

Hocks, the upper portion of the forelegs of the pig, contain by far the most meat and are delicious when long-cooked with sauerkraut or cabbage.

Knuckles, strictly speaking, are an English cut of the pork consisting of the lower part of the ham plus the hind foot. They are rarely seen in American markets. *Knuckles* with feet removed are sold in France as a *jambonneaux.*

And the *feet,* themselves (the hind feet, that is) are called *trotters.* They are meatier than the forefeet which are usually reserved for pickling.

In Italy the pigs' leg is marketed whole. Stuffed with a sausage meat called *zampone* or *zampino di Modena,* it is cooked for 3 to 4 hours and served sliced as a sort of sausage.

Two other parts of the pig worth mentioning (literally nothing is wasted) are the neckbones and the tail. You won't find much meat on these little tidbits, but cooked up with greens or kraut they add a great deal of flavor.

Pork Hocks and Sauerkraut

(4 SERVINGS)

**4 pork hocks, well scrubbed
water
1 quart sauerkraut
1 onion, thinly sliced
1 teaspoon salt
3 cloves
4 peppercorns**

Place the hocks into a large pot, cover with cold water, and bring to a boil. Turn down the heat and simmer for 1½ hours. During the process, skim as needed, and replace water that has boiled off with additional hot water added cup by cup.

Add the sauerkraut, onions, and seasonings. Continue to simmer for another hour or until hocks are fork-tender.

If you wish, you can cook the sauerkraut, onions, and seasonings separately in a pint of beer. It should cook about as long as the hocks.

Serve with apples fried in butter, rye bread or pumpernickel, and a stein of beer. Voilà, a gourmet dish, German style.

Pigs' Knuckles and Cabbage

You can load this dish with almost any vegetables you desire. Try collard greens, or turnips, for starters — or rutabaga, kale, sauerkraut, or parsnips.

(4 SERVINGS)

8 pigs' knuckles, well scrubbed
1 teaspoon salt
4 peppercorns
water
4 medium potatoes, peeled
4 small carrots
1 onion, thinly sliced
1 small head cabbage

Simmer the knuckles and seasonings in a large pot of water for 2½ hours, skimming as necessary and replacing water that has boiled off.

Add the potatoes, carrots, and onions. Simmer for ½ hour.

Add the cabbage, cut into eighths, and with hard center removed, and simmer ½ hour longer or until vegetables are done.

Serve with pumpernickel or rye bread and a stein of beer.

The good "variety" meats   125

*L*iver, heart, kidneys, sweetbreads, brains, tongue, and tripe: American butchers have a name for them and it's "varieties." The English call them "offal." But by whatever name they are known, these meats are among the best buys in the market. First, they are excellent sources of many essential nutrients. Second, they are often in less demand than other cuts of meat and, therefore, more economical.

There is a great similarity among the "varieties" of beef, veal, lamb, and pork, the main difference often being one of size (which is compatible with the size of the animal from which they come).

Most, but not all, variety meats offer an important advantage in addition to nutrition and economy: they can be quick-cooked.

Brains

Brains are delicate — and perishable. Veal brains are the highest price, but there is very little difference in the flavor or tenderness of beef, veal, lamb, or pork brains.

Precook brains before using: Simmer in hot water ½ hour, then hold under running water and slip off the membranes. Cover with boiling water, add teaspoon of salt and a teaspoon of vinegar, and simmer for 15 minutes longer. Remove, cover with cold water, and let stand for 15 minutes. Drain and use at once, or refrigerate.

Brains, once prepared as above, may be cooked in any way that sweetbreads are cooked, or as follows . . .

Fried Brains

(4 SERVINGS)

1 egg
2 tablespoons milk
1 teaspoon salt
1 pound brains, precooked (see Index) and cut into 1-inch cubes*
½ cup fine bread crumbs
1 lemon, sliced

Mix together the egg, milk, and salt and pour over the brains, stirring until brains are well coated.

Roll the brain cubes in bread crumbs and brown slowly in melted butter, using a heavy skillet.

Serve with lemon slices.

* These little brain cubes require careful handling or they will break up into pieces.

Scrambled Brains

(4 SERVINGS)

> 1 pound brains, precooked (see Index) and cut
> into ½-inch pieces
> 4 eggs, slightly beaten
> 2 tablespoons milk
> 1 teaspoon salt
> 1 tablespoon Worcestershire sauce
> 2 tablespoons butter
> 4 slices toast.

Mix together the first five ingredients and scramble in butter
until firm. Serve on toast.

127

Heart

Heart is a firm-textured meat, delicate in flavor, but grainy in texture. It rates high on the economy meat list because there is practically no waste involved. Available are veal heart (the most desirable) weighing about ¾ pound, lamb heart—about ¼ pound, pork heart—about ½ pound, and beef heart weighing 3 pounds or more.

The meat in heart is nutritious—and concentrated, 1 pound being sufficient for 4 servings.

To prepare for cooking, cut away the coarse fibers at the top and inside, cover with water containing a teaspoon or so of salt, and simmer until tender, 1 to 1½ hours for veal and lamb heart, 2 hours or more for beef and pork.

Pan-broiled Heart

(4 SERVINGS)

1 pound heart (preferably veal heart), precooked (see Index), and sliced ½ inch thick
1 teaspoon salt
½ teaspoon pepper
few grains cayenne
flour or fine bread crumbs
butter
4 slices buttered toast

Season the heart slices, dredge with flour or bread crumbs, and cook slowly in butter about 15 minutes. Serve on toast.

Stuffed Hearts

(4 SERVINGS)

2 veal hearts, with coarse fibers removed
bread stuffing (see Index)
1 teaspoon salt
¹/₂ teaspoon pepper
flour or fine bread crumbs
bacon fat
1 cup boiling water
1 tablespoon flour mixed with ¹/₄ cup water
1 tablespoon sherry

Preheat oven to 350 degrees F.

Stuff the hearts with bread stuffing, skewer together, season with salt and pepper, and dredge with flour.

Place into a casserole containing bacon fat and brown evenly on all sides.

Add 1 cup boiling water, cover, and bake for 2 hours, adding more water as the liquid cooks away.

Remove hearts to a heated platter and keep warm.

Stir into the casserole the flour mixed with water, and the sherry. Bring to a boil and pour over the hearts.

Kidneys

Kidneys are low-cost fare with a full complement of nutrients. Veal and lamb kidneys are quick and easy, requiring little cooking. Beef kidney needs to be cooked a little longer.

To prepare for cooking split and remove outer membrane, the white tubes, and the fat (scissors come in handy for this job), cover with cold water, and let stand for ½ hour. Cook kidneys quickly or stew them for a long time (at least 1 hour)—there's no in-between cooking with kidneys.

130 *Broiled Kidneys*

(4 SERVINGS)

1½ pounds veal or lamb kidneys, split and with excess fat removed
French dressing
melted butter
salt
cayenne
4 slices toast
4 slices cooked bacon

Preheat oven to 400 degrees F.

Dip the kidneys in French dressing and broil for 6 minutes about 3 inches from heat. Turn frequently.

Brush with melted butter, season with salt and cayenne, and serve on toast with a slice of bacon.

You can use fresh beef kidneys for this dish too, but broil them for about 10 minutes instead of 6.

Kidney Stew

(4 SERVINGS)

> ½ cup chopped onions
> 1 clove garlic, split
> bacon fat
> 1½ pounds beef kidneys, cut into 1½-inch cubes
>   with excess fat and white tubes removed
> flour
> ½ teaspoon salt
> freshly ground pepper
> ¾ cup dry red wine
> ¾ cup consommé

Using a heavy skillet cook the onions and garlic in the bacon fat for 1 minute.

Dredge the kidneys with flour, add to the skillet, and cook until lightly browned.

Season with salt and pepper, add the liquids, cover, and simmer about 1 hour or until kidneys are tender.

131

Kidneys en Brochette

(4 SERVINGS)

> 1½ pounds veal or lamb kidneys,* sliced and with
>   excess fat removed
> ½ pound small mushroom caps
> 4 slices bacon, cut into squares
> 3 small tomatoes, quartered
> French dressing
> salt
> cayenne

Preheat broiler.

Arrange the sliced kidneys, mushroom caps, bacon squares, and tomatoes alternately on skewers.

Broil until bacon is crisp, basting with French dressing several times.

* You can use beef kidneys for this dish too, but to be safe simmer them in bouillon for a few minutes before skewering.

Liver

Liver is one of the most nutritious of all meats, loaded with vitamin A, minerals, riboflavin, niacin, and thiamine. It's easy to buy, being marketed either fresh or frozen. And—except for calf's liver—its inexpensive. Young beef, pork, and lamb liver are tender and economical.

To prepare for cooking, remove the thin outer skin and the veins.

Sautéed Liver and Bacon

(4 SERVINGS)

8 slices bacon
salt
pepper
**1 pound liver, sliced ¼ to ½ inch thick and with
  outer skin and veins removed**
flour
2 tablespoons cream

Pan-broil the bacon in a heavy skillet, remove, and set aside.

Season the liver, dredge with flour, and sauté quickly on both sides in the bacon fat. Do not overcook—allow about 5 minutes for ½-inch slices.

Stir a little cream into the pan juices and pour over the liver.

Serve with crisp bacon.

Liver Venetian Style

This is a favorite Italian dish, served usually with rice and Parmesan cheese.

(4 SERVINGS)

4 onions, thinly sliced
2 tablespoons olive oil
1 pound liver, with outer skin and veins removed,
  cut into thin slivers
salt
pepper

Cook the onions slowly in the oil until golden. Add the liver and cook-stir about 3 minutes or until liver is browned. Season to taste.

Sweetbreads

Sweetbreads are a great delicacy. Tender and subtle in flavor, they are usually reserved for the carriage trade. Veal sweetbreads, sold separately as neck or heart sweetbreads or connected as a pair (weighing about 1 pound), are the most popular—and the most expensive too. Lamb sweetbreads, similar to those of veal are smaller but less expensive. Beef sweetbreads—not always available—are usually only neck cuts.

If the cost of sweetbreads seems high, remember that you'll only need 1 pound for 4 servings. And there's little or no waste. Marketed fresh or frozen, they provide nutritious fare and can be cooked a number of delicious ways.

To prepare sweetbreads for cooking, cover with boiling water containing a teaspoon of salt and/or a tablespoon of vinegar, and simmer—do not boil—about 20 minutes, or ½ hour for beef sweetbreads. Drain, hold under cold running water, and slip off the thin membrane. Cut out the dark tubes and thick membrane. Place under weight to flatten.

Broiled Sweetbreads

(4 SERVINGS)

**1 pound sweetbreads, prepared (see Index) and
   split
2 tablespoons flour
4 tablespoons butter
½ teaspoon salt
¼ teaspoon pepper
8 toast points**

Dredge sweetbreads lightly with flour and pan-broil in hot butter for 5 minutes on each side.

Season to taste and serve on buttered toast points.

Braised Sweetbreads

(4 SERVINGS)

3 tablespoons butter
1 pound sweetbreads, prepared (see Index) and
  sliced
1/4 pound mushrooms sliced
1 1/2 tablespoons flour
1 cup chicken broth or water
1 tablespoon sherry
4 slices toast

Melt the butter in a heavy skillet and brown the sweetbreads
and mushrooms on all sides.

Sprinkle in flour and stir in broth. Stir and simmer 5 minutes.
Add the sherry. Serve on toast.

Sautéed Sweetbreads

(4 SERVINGS)

1 pound sweetbreads, prepared (see Index)
4 tablespoons butter
1/2 cup water
1/2 teaspoon salt
1/4 teaspoon pepper
lemon juice

Pan-fry sweetbreads in butter until brown on all sides (about
5 minutes), remove to heated platter. Add water to pan, season
with a little salt and pepper and a squeeze of lemon juice,
boil up, and spoon over sweetbreads.

Baked Sweetbreads

(4 SERVINGS)

> 1 pound sweetbreads, prepared (see Index) and sliced
> salt
> pepper
> flour
> 2 tablespoons melted butter
> 3 thin slices salt pork (or bacon)

Preheat oven to 450 degrees F.

Season the sweetbreads with salt and pepper, dredge with flour, place into a casserole, and brush with melted butter.

Cover with sliced pork and bake 25 minutes, basting from time to time with the pan juices.

Creamed Sweetbreads

(4 SERVINGS)

> 1 pound sweetbreads, prepared (see Index) and cut into small pieces
> 1 cup cream sauce or velouté sauce (see Index)
> salt
> nutmeg
> pepper
> 4 slices toast or 4 patty shells

Cook the sweetbreads in the sauce at low heat for 2 minutes. Season to taste and serve on toast points or patty shells. Vary by adding chopped ham or chicken—or sautéed mushrooms (but you'll need to double the amount of the sauce).

Tongue

Marketed fresh, smoked, corned, pickled, or canned tongue is a handy and economical meat that can be served either hot or cold. It is a solid meat with practically no waste yielding 4 to 6 servings per pound.

Beef tongue (2 to 5 pounds) is sold fresh, smoked, cured, or cooked in ready-to-serve packages, in cans, and in jars. Veal tongue weighs from 1/2 to 2 pounds and is available only as freshly butchered meat. Lamb tongues are small, usually weighing only about 1/4 pound each. They are usually pickled, but are often available fresh. Pork tongues, which weigh anywhere from 1/2 to 1 1/4 pounds, are almost always precooked and sold as "lunch meat."

To cook fresh tongue, first scrub with warm water. Then cover with boiling water, add a slice of onion, a bay leaf, a teaspoon salt, a few peppercorns, and a few cloves. Cover and simmer until tender (2 to 4 hours), depending upon size. Drain, immerse in cold water, slit, and peel off the skin. Cut away the bones and gristle at the thick end.

To cook pickled or smoked tongue, follow the directions on the wrapper. When serving hot tongue, slice it about 1/4 inch thick. Cold tongue should be sliced more thinly.

Braised Tongue

(4 SERVINGS)

1 1-pound veal tongue, cooked and prepared (see Index)
1/4 cup diced carrots
1/4 cup diced celery
1/4 cup chopped onion
4 tablespoons butter
4 tablespoons flour
3 cups bouillon or liquid in which tongue was cooked
1 cup tomato juice
1 teaspoon salt
1/2 teaspoon pepper
1 tablespoon Worcestershire sauce

Preheat oven to 300 degrees F.

Put the tongue and vegetables into a baking dish.

In a small skillet, melt the butter, brown the flour, stir in the liquids, and season with salt, pepper, and Worcestershire.

Pour the sauce over the tongue and vegetables, cover, and bake 1 hour, turning the tongue once.

Sweet and Sour Tongue

(4 SERVINGS)

1 onion, thinly sliced
1/2 lemon, thinly sliced
1/2 cup bouillon
1/2 cup vinegar
1/2 cup raisins
1/2 cup brown sugar
1 bay leaf
4 whole cloves
1/2 teaspoon salt
few grains cayenne
1 pound veal tongue, prepared and cooked (see Index) and cut into thin slices

Place the onion, lemon, bouillon, vinegar, raisins, sugar, and seasonings into a shallow pan and simmer 10 minutes.

Add the tongue slices and heat thoroughly.

Tripe

Tripe is a favorite dish in France, and very popular in England as a breakfast dish. It is inexpensive and easy to cook, though requiring a little time. There are three kinds: honeycomb, (the choicest), pocket, and smooth. It is marketed fresh, canned, or pickled.

To cook tripe, simply cover with water, add a tablespoon salt, and simmer 1½ hours or until tender.

Broiled Tripe

(4 SERVINGS)

1 pound fresh tripe, cooked (see Index) and cut into serving pieces—about 5 x 7 inches
salt
pepper
flour
½ cup melted butter
dry bread crumbs

Season tripe with salt and pepper, sprinkle on both sides with flour, then dip in melted butter. Sprinkle on both sides with bread crumbs.

Broil 3 or 4 inches from the heat until brown, turn, and repeat on other side.

Serve as is or make a mixed grill by adding broiled bacon and broiled tomatoes.

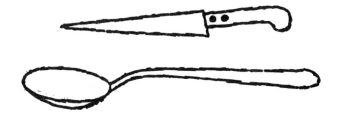

Tripe and Onions

(4 SERVINGS)

1 pound fresh tripe, cooked (see Index) and cut into small pieces
2 cups milk
3 onions, chopped
1 bay leaf
1 teaspoon salt
½ teaspoon pepper
2 tablespoons butter
2 tablespoons flour
3 slices bacon, cooked and crumbled

Put the tripe, milk, onions, and seasonings into a saucepan. Cover and simmer for ½ hour or until tripe is tender. Strain off the liquid.

In a skillet melt the butter, stir in the flour, cook for 1 minute, then add some of the milk from the tripe. Stir to make a smooth sauce.

Stir the cream sauce into the tripe and sprinkle with crumbled bacon.

S ausage is made by grinding bits of meat—mostly from the shoulder—left over after the animal has been butchered. Sausage is usually made from pork, but it may—and often does—contain beef, veal, and mutton, as well.

Sausage meat is marketed loose or in links made by stuffing the ground meat into casings of intestine. It is sold fresh, frozen, dried, or smoked. Fresh pork sausage is very, very perishable requiring careful refrigeration.

In cooking loose sausage meat, you simply form cakes or patties and fry until well done, turning once or twice during the process. Link sausage should be started with a little water in the pan to keep the casings from bursting. As the water cooks away the links will brown nicely. Cook until the pink disappears—never undercook.

Sausages of all kinds make an excellent and inexpensive meal served hot or cold with potatoes, noodles, macaroni, spaghetti, hominy, corn meal mush, or fruit.

What makes sausage so interesting is the infinite variety of seasonings—and combinations of seasonings—used in different countries of the world, and in different regions of the countries.

On a recent trip around the world we were able to sample many sausages not easy to get in the United States: Little dried beef sausages in Japan and their counterpart hanging in the markets of Hong Kong; hot sausages relished by Southeast Asians (we ate them in Bangkok); the relatively mild dried Indian sausages in Delhi; tangy and flavorful sausages made of mutton scraps sold in the markets of old Athens; the almost countless varieties of Italian sausages; the many saucissons of France; the chorizos and related types of Spanish and Portuguese sausages.

Sausages of the world that are generally available in American markets are as follows:

Blutwurst—a German sausage made with blood, well seasoned and cooked in the casing.

Bologna—a large-sized sausage originating in Italy and made from mixed meats and spices.

Bratwurst—a German sausage made from pork scraps well seasoned with herbs and spices.

Chorizo—(from Spain and Latin America)—little red sausages made from pork, highly flavored with red pepper, and smoked.

Coteghino—an Italian pork sausage, dried and smoked.

Frankfurter—(of German origin)—made from forcemeat composed of lean beef, often with a little pork added. Frankfurters are always smoked.

Kielbasa—a Polish sausage made from lean pork and fat bound by blood, flavored with pimentos and cloves, dried and smoked.

Knackwurst (also called *knockwurst* or *knoblauch*)—a beef and pork sausage seasoned with cumin and garlic dried and smoked.

Liverwurst (Braunschweiger)—a sort of liver pudding.

Mortadella—a large salami-like sausage of Italian extraction.

Pepperoni—Italian version of chorizo.

Salami—Italian mixed-meat sausage, usually, but not always, flavored with garlic.

Scrapple—not really a sausage but closely related. A specialty of Pennsylvania Dutch country, made from bits of pork shoulder and liver mixed with corn meal, onions, and herbs.

Sulze—a German head cheese—scraps of pigs' head in aspic.

Sweet (and hot) Italian sausage—fresh pork sausage seasoned with orégano (the hot sausage is laced with cayenne).

Thuringer (cervelat)—a kind of German summer sausage.

Vienna sausage—small frankfurter.

Chorizos

The "little red sausages" made from pork and highly flavored with red pepper are found wherever Spanish is spoken—in Europe, in Mexico, in Puerto Rico, and in the Central American countries. And, of course, they are plentiful in the United States in Latin American neighborhoods.

Chorizos are sliced and eaten cold as tapas *or hors d'oeuvres, or in combination with other meats as a lunch or supper dish. Add them to beans, chic peas,* paella, *Puerto Rican chicken to impart extra flavor. Cook them with eggs and omelets, or use them in almost any recipe calling for hot sausage.*

Coteghino with Lentils

Coteghino, one of the big dried sausages you see hanging in Italian specialty stores, come in two sizes: 1-pound links and ¼-pound links. They're very popular with the Italian boiled dinner called bollito misto *and especially delicious cooked with lentils for which they seem to have a special affinity.*

(4 SERVINGS)

½ pound dried lentils
water
1 pound coteghino sausage

Pick over and wash the lentils thoroughly and put into a 4-quart pan with enough water to cover.

Wash the sausage and place on top of the lentils, bring to a boil, partially covered, then simmer for 1½ hours or until the lentils are soft and have absorbed all the water.

Peel the skins from the sausages and cut into ½-inch slices.

Serve the lentils topped with the coteghino slices.

144 *Italian Sausages with Peppers*

The Italians are famous for their sausages, there being countless varieties. Those we in this country are most familiar with—and those most available—are sweet sausage and hot sausage.

Sweet and hot sausages cook quickly and are delicious served with almost anything, but especially with highly flavored food such as green peppers, zucchini (squash), tomatoes, and artichokes. The latter, very popular in Italy, are grown all winter in most parts of the country and are harvested while still small.

(4 SERVINGS)

2 Italian sausages (sweet or hot)
6 green peppers, seeded and cut into eighths
½ teaspoon salt
¼ teaspoon pepper

Place the sausages into a heavy skillet, cook over low heat, turning once or twice, until browned on all sides.

Season the peppers with salt and pepper. Add them to the skillet. Cook on both sides until brown and tender (enough fat will have accumulated in the pan to fry them nicely).

Serve with spaghetti or macaroni and Italian bread.

Italian Sausages with Tomatoes

This simple dish, quick and easy to prepare, will surprise you with its delightful combination of flavors — the sausages and artichokes seem to be made for each other. Inexpensive too.

(4 SERVINGS)

8 Italian sausages (sweet or hot)
½ teaspoon salt
¼ teaspoon pepper
8 frozen artichoke hearts

Place the sausages into a heavy skillet, cook over low heat, turning once or twice, until browned on all sides.

Add the artichokes to the skillet. Cook until browned all over and serve with spaghetti or macaroni.

Kielbasa (Polish Sausage) and Sauerkraut

(4 SERVINGS)

1 quart sauerkraut
1 (10-ounce) can beer or 5 ounces dry white wine combined with 5 ounces water
1 onion, sliced
½ teaspoon salt
freshly ground pepper
1 kielbasa loop

Put the sauerkraut into a saucepan with the liquid (you can use water only, if you wish), the onions, and the seasonings, cover and cook at a simmer for 1 hour.

Meanwhile, slice the kielbasa diagonally into 1½-inch pieces, toss into a hot skillet, and cook, turning, until browned on all sides.

Pour off most of the accumulated fat, add the sauerkraut, stir, and cover. Cook over very low heat for about 10 minutes.

Pork Sausages and Fried Apples

(4 SERVINGS)

water
**2 pounds link sausage (4 or 8 links depending
upon size)**
**8 apples, peeled, cored, and sliced about $\frac{1}{4}$ inch
thick**
$\frac{1}{2}$ teaspoon salt
$\frac{1}{4}$ teaspoon pepper

Cover the bottom of a heavy skillet with water. Add the
sausage links and cook over medium heat, turning frequently,
about $\frac{1}{2}$ hour or until sausages are browned.

Remove to a heated serving dish.

Fry the apples quickly in the sausage fat until browned. Turn
once.

Drain the apples on a paper towel, season, add to the sausages,
and serve hot.

Sauces and stuffings   147

*T*he difference between an ordinary run-of-the-kitchen meal and a memorable dining experience is very often an imaginative sauce. So important are sauces to professional chefs that most substantial restaurants and hotels employ sauciers — men whose talents are devoted exclusively to the creation of such culinary accompaniments.

Cooks in the home fixing economy meals are all too often apt to forget all about sauces — and just at the time when they might prove all the more useful.

In this chapter we offer a few not-too-complicated sauces that you can make without throwing your budget out of joint.

Back Yard Barbecue Sauce

(YIELDS ABOUT 1½ CUPS)

¼ **cup melted butter**
¼ **cup vinegar**
¼ **cup chili sauce**
¼ **cup Worcestershire sauce**
¼ **cup lemon juice**
1 clove garlic, crushed
1 medium onion, chopped
dash Tabasco
½ **teaspoon salt**
½ **teaspoon freshly ground pepper**

Mix all the ingredients together in a small saucepan and simmer a few minutes.

Quick Barbecue Sauce

(YIELDS ABOUT 2 CUPS)

1 cup catsup
½ **cup vinegar**
½ **cup water**
½ **cup melted butter**
2 tablespoons Worcestershire sauce
2 teaspoons butter

Mix all the ingredients together in a small saucepan and simmer a minute or so to blend.

Southwest Barbecue Sauce

(YIELDS ABOUT 2 CUPS)

1 clove garlic, crushed
1 medium onion, chopped
1/4 cup butter
1 teaspoon brown sugar
1 teaspoon dry mustard
1 teaspoon paprika
1 teaspoon chili powder
1 teaspoon salt
1 1/2 cups water
1/4 cup vinegar
1 tablespoon Worcestershire sauce

Cook the garlic and onions in the butter for 1 minute or so, then stir in all the dry ingredients. Add the liquids and simmer about 15 minutes.

Béchamel Sauce (Basic White Sauce)

(YIELDS 1 CUP)

2 tablespoons butter
2 tablespoons flour
1 cup milk or half and half
salt
pepper
dash nutmeg

Using a small saucepan, melt the butter, stir in the flour, and blend well. Stir in the milk, bring slowly to the boiling point, and cook 2 minutes, stirring constantly. Season to taste.

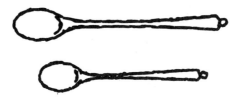

Velouté Sauce

(YIELDS 1 CUP)

Make Béchamel sauce (see Index) substituting a cup of chicken stock for milk. When the sauce is made stir in ⅓ cup cream.

Béarnaise Sauce

(YIELDS ABOUT 1 CUP)

2 tablespoons chopped shallots
½ cup dry white wine
1½ teaspoons dried tarragon
1 bay leaf
sprig parsley
½ teaspoon freshly ground pepper
few grains cayenne
½ teaspoon salt
5 egg yolks
¾ cup melted butter

Into a small saucepan put the shallots, wine, and seasonings. Bring to a boil and cook until reduced to about 2 tablespoons of liquid. Strain and cool.

Put the cooled tarragon mixture into the bowl of a blender and blend at high speed for 10 seconds. Add the warm butter and blend again slowly until sauce thickens. (If sauce becomes too thick, add a teaspoon or so of hot water and blend again.)

Quick Béarnaise Sauce

(YIELDS ABOUT 1½ CUPS)

2 tablespoons tarragon vinegar
2 tablespoons dry white wine (optional)
½ teaspoon grated onion
1 teaspoon dried tarragon
2 tablespoons butter
1 cup mayonnaise
1 egg yolk, beaten

Simmer the vinegar, wine, onion, tarragon, and butter for a few minutes in a small saucepan.

Heat the mayonnaise in a double boiler and gradually stir in the vinegar mixture. Add the egg yolk and beat until thickened.

Bordelaise Sauce

(YIELDS ABOUT 1 CUP)

2 tablespoons butter
2 tablespoons minced shallots, or spring onions
1/2 cup dry red wine
1/2 cup beef bouillon
2 teaspoons chopped parsley
2 teaspoons lemon juice
1 teaspoon salt
few grains cayenne

Using a small saucepan melt the butter, add the shallots, and simmer about 1 minute.

Add the wine and bouillon and simmer down to about half.

Add the remaining ingredients and simmer about 3 minutes longer.

Brown Tomato Sauce

(YIELDS ABOUT 1 1/2 CUPS)

2 tablespoons butter
2 tablespoons flour
1 cup strained crushed tomatoes, chopped
1 teaspoon meat glaze dissolved in 1/2 cup hot water or beef extract
1/2 teaspoon salt
1/4 teaspoon pepper

Brown the butter in a small saucepan, stir in the flour and gradually add the remaining ingredients. Simmer about 10 minutes.

Mushroom Sauce

(YIELDS ABOUT 1½ CUPS)

2 tablespoons butter
1 tablespoon finely chopped shallots or spring onions
1 cup thinly sliced mushrooms
1 teaspoon lemon juice
1 teaspoon meat glaze dissolved in ½ cup hot water or beef extract

Melt the butter in a small saucepan, add the shallots and mushrooms, and simmer for about 5 minutes. Mix in all the other ingredients and simmer 1 minute longer.

Mustard Sauce

(YIELDS ABOUT ½ CUP)

2 tablespoons melted butter
1 teaspoon dry mustard
1 teaspoon Worcestershire sauce
1 tablespoon Sauce Diable
1 tablespoon cream

Mix together the butter, mustard, Worcestershire, and Sauce Diable in a saucepan and heat. Add the cream and stir until thickish.

Skillet Sauce

(YIELDS ABOUT ½ CUP)

2 tablespoons butter
1 teaspoon flour
½ cup water
½ teaspoon salt
½ teaspoon freshly ground pepper

When the meat has been removed from the skillet, pour off most of any fat that may have accumulated. Add butter, stir in the flour, scraping from the bottom of the pan the coagulated meat essence. Add water, season, simmer for 1 minute, and pour over the meat.

Basic Bread Stuffing

(YIELDS 2 CUPS)

2 cups diced stale bread
¼ cup melted butter or bacon fat or sausage drip-
ping
½ teaspoon salt
¼ teaspoon pepper
1 small onion, minced

Mix all the ingredients together lightly.

For a more savory dressing add a pinch of sage, a bit of celery seed, ½ cup extra of minced onion, or chopped chives, or chopped green pepper or pimento.

New England Stuffing

(YIELDS 2 CUPS)

2 cups coarse dry toast crumbs
water or beef bouillon
1-inch cube salt pork, finely chopped, or a little
sausage meat
1 egg, beaten
½ teaspoon salt
¼ teaspoon pepper

Moisten the toast crumbs with water or bouillon and mix in the remaining ingredients.

Sausage Stuffing

(YIELDS 2 CUPS)

¹/₄ **pound sausage meat**
2 cups dry bread crumbs or bread cubes
¹/₂ **teaspoon minced parsley**
¹/₂ **tablespoon minced onion**
¹/₂ **teaspoon salt**
¹/₄ **teaspoon pepper**

Cook, stirring, the sausage until brown, then mix in the remaining ingredients.

154

Dumplings for Stews

(4 SERVINGS)

1¹/₂ **cups flour**
3¹/₂ **teaspoons baking powder**
¹/₂ **teaspoon salt**
³/₄ **cup milk**
1 egg (optional)

Sift flour, baking powder, and salt into a mixing bowl. Add the milk and egg and stir well. Drop by spoonfuls onto the boiling stew and cover the pot for 15 minutes, *do not uncover* while the dumplings are cooking. The pot cover should fit well enough to hold the steam. It is the steam that cooks the top of the dumplings.

Index

155

156

157

RELATIVE COSTS OF MEAT CUTS

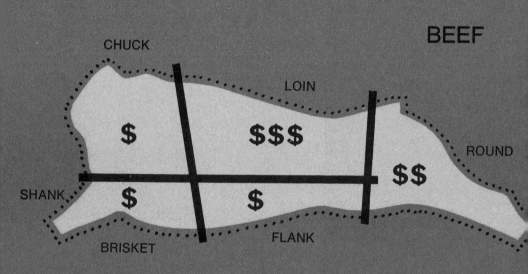

BEEF

CHUCK

LOIN

$

$$$

ROUND

SHANK

$

$

$$

FLANK

BRISKET

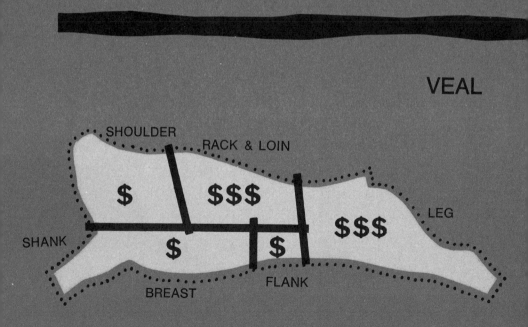

VEAL

SHOULDER

RACK & LOIN

$

$$$

LEG

SHANK

$

$

$$$

BREAST

FLANK